LINDBERGH IN MONTANA
An Air Adventurer Leaves a Legacy in the Treasure State

Dennis Gaub

Treasure State Heritage Press

BILLINGS, MONTANA

Copyright © 2022 by Dennis Gaub

All rights reserved. No part of this publication may be reproduced, distributed or transmitted in any form or by any means, without prior written permission.

**Treasure State Heritage Press
Billings, Montana 59101
www.treasurestatepress.com**

Book Layout © 2014 BookDesignTemplates.com

Lindbergh in Montana/ Dennis Gaub -- 1st ed.
ISBN 978-1-7338736-2-8

LCCN - 2022918719

This book is dedicated to early pioneers in the Montana sky who blazed the trail to modern air travel.

What's Inside

Foreword	1
Introduction	5
1-The life of a flier begins	11
2-Lindbergh's first flight	19
3-Heading to Montana	27
4-Treasure State thrills	33
5-Flying at the fairs	41
6-Boating the Yellowstone River	49
7-A plane of his own	55
8-Flying with father	63
9-The break he needed	67
10-Flying the mail	75
11-The Atlantic beckons	81
12-Taking Butte by storm	89
13-Great Falls gala	101
14-Helena hubbub	105
15-Back to Billings	115
16-Escape into the Montana mountains	123
17-"A thing of beauty"	131
18-1928	137
19-A question of loyalty	141
20-War and peace	155
21-Casting a shadow in Montana	159
22-Death at "my home"	171
23-Still a Montana presence	175
24-Echoes of the kidnapping in Montana	185
Conclusion	189
Photos	193
Acknowledgements	205
Sources	209

Index 219

Foreword

As I write this in 2022, ninety-five years have passed since Charles Lindbergh dazzled the world. In May 1927, he became the most famous person on the planet, the first media-developed hero of the modern era, when he completed the first solo airplane flight across the Atlantic. He flew the *Spirit of St. Louis* from New York to Paris, a 3,600-mile trip, in thirty-three and a half hours. That seems slow today when jets travel from the United States to Europe in ten or eleven hours, yet this was a little more than two decades after the Wright Brothers' first flight. What Lindbergh accomplished made him the toast of kings, presidents, business leaders, and regular people across the globe.

News of Lindbergh's feat ushered in the modern era of media-driven fame and instant celebrity status for those whose accomplishments captivate the public. Baby Boomers like me need only think of the Beatles' arrival on American shores in 1964, followed by their appearance on The Ed Sullivan Show, to imagine what greeted Lindbergh. Or we can think back to the tragedy of John Kennedy's assassination the year before in Dallas to get a comparable sense of an event so big that all else pales in comparison. Those of us in that generation can all remember where we were and what we were doing when time seemed to stand still.

Almost everyone who was alive in 1927 is gone now, but Lindbergh's instant fame created the template for later, similarly high-profile events.

Lindbergh, then twenty-five years old, lived forty-seven more years, until his death from cancer in 1974. During his lifetime, people in many U.S. localities, as well as in other countries, got ample opportunities to see him close up and from afar. He became a citizen of the world.

As a Montana native, though, I argue that the Treasure State can make as strong a claim on Lindbergh as one of its own as any place on earth, except three other states: his home state of Minnesota; Nebraska, where he learned to fly and which he saw from the air during a 1922 barnstorming tour; and Missouri, where St. Louis businessmen financed the plane, named for that city in gratitude, that Lindbergh used for his trans-Atlantic flight. Lindbergh first came to Montana as a wing walker and a parachute jumper with a barnstorming group a century ago, in 1922. He and his colleagues performed at fairs in Billings and Lewistown, and he lived in the Magic City for three months. While in Billings, Lindbergh worked as mechanic, fixing car and airplane engines, at a garage owned by Bob and Edward Westover.

Then, after the 1927 New York-to-Paris flight, Lindbergh embarked on a tour to boost commercial aviation. Flying his Spirit plane, he visited all of the then forty-eight states. In Montana, he stopped in Butte and Helena, attracting massive crowds in both cities. He also flew over Great Falls and Missoula, soaring over the latter city on the way to his Spokane tour stop. Billings evidently remained dear in his heart because he went hundreds of miles out of his way to fly over the bustling city instead of flying a direct sixty-six miles from Helena to Butte.

Lindbergh visited Montana again in 1939 when war clouds were building over Europe and Asia. He was on a nationwide tour for the Army to review military aviation facilities. Flying across the Treasure State from west to east, he stopped in Missoula and

Billings, where he renewed his acquaintance with Bob Westover.

The famed flyer made numerous under-the-radar trips to Montana from the mid-1960s on. These journeys were prompted by his desire to visit his son, Land, who with his brother Jon had purchased a western Montana ranch. Lindbergh's growing conservation advocacy resulted in his being invited to Helena in February 1972, when he spoke to delegates of Montana's state constitutional convention. The resulting landmark constitution, ratified by Montana voters that year, contains some of the strongest conservation and environmental protection wording of any state constitution.

All said, I believe that Lindbergh's time in Montana deserves a book of its own. Lindbergh won a Pulitzer Prize for his account of the flight across the Atlantic. And A. Scott Berg's Pulitzer-winning 1998 biography of Lindbergh remains the gold standard of books about this man's fascinating, complicated, and often controversial life.

Thus, you will not read another Lindbergh biography, although this book outlines the highlights of his life from his birth in Little Falls, Minnesota, in 1902, to his death seventy-two years later on the island of Maui. Instead, Lindbergh in Montana represents my attempt to tell the story of his time in the state and to determine as best I can how he was shaped by the state I've called home for seven decades.

Introduction

"He has been called the last American hero. He disliked such sobriquets, yet one can only conclude that Charles Lindbergh was a leader without followers. His life...is altogether singular, but profoundly characteristic. There cannot be another like it."

William Jovanovich, foreword, *Charles Lindbergh: Autobiography of Values*, 1977

Sobriquet. An alias or a nickname. "The last American hero" is a fitting way to describe Charles Lindbergh's life for almost five decades after his solo flight across the Atlantic in May 1927, in the *Spirit of St. Louis*. It was an accomplishment that stopped the hearts of millions in the United States and around the world. Yet five years before perhaps the first true media event of the modern era, Charles Lindbergh was not a hero. He came to Montana as a lanky, unknown twenty-year-old, the only son of a quixotic Republican congressman who represented a Minnesota district, and as a dropout from the University of Wisconsin.

By 1922, the flying bug had bitten him, and he wanted to pilot an airplane. He had flown a plane with an instructor but was unable to fly solo because he couldn't post the damage bond required by the plane owner at the flying school he attended in Lincoln, Nebraska. So, Lindbergh hitched his star to a barnstorming group that took off from Lincoln, a city that was an early aviation hotspot. He first cleaned the barnstorming airplane, then, to attract more people to pay for short flights on the plane, he began performing as a parachute jumper and wing walker. Along with pilot J.H. "Jack" Lynch (nicknamed "Cupid"); the plane's owner, Kansas rancher "Banty" Rogers; and the group's companion dog, a fox terrier named Booster, Lindbergh arrived in Billings, Montana, in the summer of 1922.

It was during that time that Lindbergh became known as "Slim," a handle that persisted in Montana's Magic City even when the rest of the country called him "Lucky Lindy" or "The Lone Eagle."

Was Lindbergh a leader without followers, as his longtime publisher William Jovanovich called him? Maybe so in Montana. Yet he carved a legacy that continues. It can be seen in the preamble and list of inalienable rights of Montana's 1972 Constitution, words that say Treasure State residents have the right to a clean and safe environment. When Lindbergh addressed the delegates of the convention as they drafted the constitution, he did not advocate specific language in the document but shared his global perspective on conservation and the need for Montana to preserve its relatively unspoiled terrain. His words influenced convention delegates, who included strong environmental wording in the state's overarching law.

Lindbergh's legacy, something that goes well beyond airplanes and flight, can also be felt along Montana's Blackfoot River Valley. There, Land Lindbergh, the second-oldest son of Charles and Anne Morrow Lindbergh, began ranching in 1965 in partnership with Land's older brother, Jon. Land Lindbergh, born in 1937, eighty-five years old in 2002, and a retired rancher, has been involved in conservation efforts over the years, including the Blackfoot Challenge and the Nature Conservancy.

When Lindbergh first came to the Treasure State, he built a reputation as a wing walker and parachute jumper, part of a barnstorming outfit that performed in Nebraska, Kansas, Colorado, and Wyoming before it reached Montana.

Lynch, Rogers, and Lindbergh flew over what was then called Custer's Battlefield, now the Little Bighorn Battlefield, and put on a show in the south-central Montana town of Hardin. From there, it was a short flight of less than fifty miles to Billings, where Lindbergh lived about three months before he returned to Lincoln.

Lindbergh was so unknown that when he first came to Montana, articles about the Lynch-led barnstormers published in the *Billings Gazette* twice misspelled his name. And Lindbergh's adventure in Billings nearly went awry. Lynch began flying for Lloyd Lamb, a Billings man; Rogers found another pilot for his plane and returned to Kansas; and Lindbergh no longer had a job.

He seems to have been resourceful, though, because he found work with two former Nebraskans, the Westover brothers. They owned a repair garage on First Avenue North in Billings that fixed cars and airplanes and was one of the first auto-towing businesses in town. The flying bug had bitten the Westovers, too, and they owned a Lincoln Standard airplane. Good early marketers, they, and pilots they hired, flew the plane with banners advertising the garage.

The Westovers must have decided that Lindbergh's parachute-jumping and wing walking skills would boost business at their barnstorming exhibitions in the Midland Empire, as the Billings trade area was known. They took him along. The charge for someone to "hop" a ride on the plane was ten dollars, and business was never brisk. The aviation entrepreneurs, Lindbergh among them, had to improvise to generate revenue that barely paid expenses. Westover and his young associate sometimes took a collection when Lindbergh jumped or when stunt flying occurred.

Lindbergh didn't leave Billings much richer than when he came, and there was no fame to chase in 1922. He pursued his aviation passion in those three months in Montana in relative anonymity. The decades of his being the most celebrated person in the world still lay ahead, although after he rocketed to renown in 1927, some Billings people would incorrectly claim they flew with him during after his summer in their city.

Lindbergh and his fellow Lincoln barnstormers worked their way across Kansas, into Colorado and Wyoming, and reached Billings by late August 1922. They performed in and near an already booming city of about 20,000 people (nicknamed the Magic City because of its explosive growth). Lindbergh and pilot J.H. "Cupid" Lynch got a slot at the Midland Empire Fair, where they dipped and dashed through the air above the Yellowstone River. Then, when fairgoers in the stands at the grounds seemed sufficiently mesmerized, Lynch and Lindbergh took off in their Lincoln Standard plane and headed to an early airfield west of Billings. The airstrip is long gone now, its place taken by a Billings West End retail complex that is among the largest in Montana, and the pied pipers of the time— Lynch and Lindbergh—got some business but not enough to get rich. They probably paid for gas, food and lodging—most of those tabs—but were left with little more in their wallets or jingling in their pockets.

Working a crowd drawn to the Hogan air strip, Lynch began taking people up for short flights. Lindbergh's job was to collect fees from passengers, many of them awaiting their first ride in an airplane.

Lynch and Lindbergh also performed in September 1922 at the Central Montana Fair in Lewistown, and Lindbergh spent several weeks working as an airplane and auto engine mechanic in Billings. Finally in October, his time in Montana finished, Lindbergh needed to get back to Lincoln. He could have taken a conventional trip back by buying a ticket on a train for one of the three railroads that served Billings, but Lindbergh sought more adventure. Using a leaky boat he had purchased for a pittance, he put into the Yellowstone River in Billings, intending to follow the water route of the Yellowstone and Missouri Rivers to his destination, but he got only about twenty miles downstream. Cold fall rain and the constant need to bail out water forced him to scuttle his attempt to mimic Lewis and Clark.

A farm family east of Billings saw Lindbergh and gave him a night's lodging and a meal, then he returned to Billings and caught a train to Lincoln. The boys in that farm family learned five or six years later, after Lindbergh's 1927 flight, that they had helped his passage to legendary status.

Lindbergh wasn't finished with Montana. After his New York-to-Paris flight, he took off in the Spirit of St. Louis on a nationwide odyssey to boost commercial flight. He came to Montana, stopped in Helena and Butte, and flew over Billings, Missoula, and Great Falls, dropping notes in those cities that expressed his regret at being unable to land because his itinerary was packed.

All this preceded Lindbergh's storybook marriage to Ann Morrow, the death of their first-born child at the hands of a kidnapper, and Lindbergh's controversial stance in opposition to President Franklin Roosevelt as the drums of war rumbled in 1941.

Among the states where Lindbergh developed into an airman, Montana ranks high, and Billings stands out for the amount of time that a young man called "Slim" spent there.

Did Lindbergh's first visit to Montana help shape him for a future as arguably the first hero in the media spotlight of the modern age? Maybe yes, maybe no. It's impossible to answer that question. Yet there can be no doubt that Montana left its mark on Charles Lindbergh, and Lindbergh left his mark on Montana.

First, however, the Lindbergh story starts in Detroit, where he was born; heads to Little Falls, Minnesota, where he spent much of his growing-up years on his father's farm; and continues on to Washington, D.C., where the senior Lindbergh served five terms in Congress.

ONE

The life of a flier begins

Charles Lindbergh may have felt comfortable in Billings because of his own largely small-town upbringing. Born in Detroit on February 4, 1902—his mother, Evangeline, hailed from there—he spent his early growing-up years on the family farm, on the western bank of the Mississippi River, two miles south of Little Falls, Minnesota. The town, near the geographic center of the state, had a population of about 5,800 in 1900, and it was where Lindbergh's father, also named Charles, practiced law.

The senior Lindbergh became interested in politics and was elected to Congress in 1906, representing Minnesota's Sixth District for ten years as a Republican. The future flier's mother, Evangeline Land, was born in in Detroit, the daughter of a prominent family there and in nearby Ontario. Evangeline Lindbergh, who earned an undergraduate degree from the University of Michigan and a graduate degree from Columbia University in New York City, was a schoolteacher for most of her adult life.

Congressman Lindbergh, a widower who had remarried, and his second wife, Evangeline, separated in 1910 but never divorced. They lived mostly separate lives, the lawyer and solon in Washington, D. C., and Little Falls, and Evangeline in Detroit.

In his 1927 book, *We*, the younger Charles Lindbergh recalled living mostly in Minnesota for the first four years of his life. Then, when his father was elected to Congress, he seldom spent more than a few months in the same place. He lived in Washington during winter months and in Minnesota during the summer. He occasionally visited Detroit to see his mother and her family.

At the age of eight, Lindbergh entered the private Force School in Washington. He said later that his education was irregular because his parents constantly moved. Until he entered the University of Wisconsin, Lindbergh had never attended a school for a full year. He attended public and private schools from Washington to California and enrolled in Redondo Union High School in Redondo Beach, California, but moved before graduating there.

"My chief interest in school lay along mechanical lines," Lindbergh said. Thus, after graduating from Little Falls High School, he decided to try mechanical engineering and enrolled in the University of Wisconsin's college of engineering.

That brought Lindbergh to Madison, Wisconsin, and he soon became "intensely interested" in aviation. He saw an airplane for the first time near Washington in 1912. Although flying fascinated Lindbergh, it wasn't until 1922, when he enrolled in a flying school, that he got close enough to a plane to touch it.

Lindbergh had been raised around guns at his Minnesota home, so he joined the Reserve Officer Training Corps program at the start of his freshman year at UW. He said he spent every spare minute when not studying in the shooting gallery and on the range.

Lindbergh fulfilled his ROTC obligation after his freshman year by participating in artillery school at Camp Knox, Kentucky. Then he steered his motorcycle south, with forty-eight dollars in his pocket and Florida as his destination. The day after he arrived in

Jacksonville, he started back to the Midwest but by a different route west of where he had traveled to Florida. He returned to Madison with nine dollars left, driving a motorcycle that badly needed repairs. He overhauled the engine and drove to Little Falls, where he spent the rest of his vacation.

By the time his third semester at UW was underway, Lindbergh had decided to study aeronautics in earnest. As he got deeper into his study of the subject, he decided that aviation had a promising future.

"I intended to take it up as a life work," he said in *We* .

Lindbergh got to the halfway point of his sophomore year at the UW, then he embarked on the path of life—flying—that would make him one of the most storied people of the twentieth century. He dropped out of school, got on his motorcycle again, and headed to Lincoln, Nebraska, where he enrolled as a flying student with the Nebraska Aircraft Corporation.

In *We*, Lindbergh noted that not all roads in Wisconsin were paved in March 1922. It was slow going, so Lindbergh hailed a passing farm wagon. He got a ride to a railroad station and shipped his motorcycle by rail to Lincoln, a place that formed his destiny as much as anywhere.

In fact, Billings might never have been able to list Lindbergh among its famous people had it not been for Lincoln. If the Nebraska state capital had not become such an aviation hotbed in the early 1920s, attracting Lindbergh and prompting him to take flying lessons there, would he have latched onto the barnstorming outfit that brought him to Billings?

Impossible to answer, but by 1920, Lincoln residents were being enticed into sky travel, their magic carpet an early biplane. A newspaper advertisement invited readers to see their city from the air.

"Passenger flight(s) will be given in a two- passenger Lincoln Standard Plane, from the Nebraska Aircraft Corporation flying field, near the Nee Hebb Motor plant" that Sunday at three p.m., the ad read. I. O. Biffle, a test pilot for the company, would be at the controls.

Another newspaper ad beckoned visitors to the Nebraska State Fair in Lincoln to take a "Joy Ride in Cloudland" aboard a Lincoln Standard Tourabout. For ten to twenty-five dollars, brave souls could take to the sky with Biffle or another corporation pilot, E. V. Gardner.

The ad assured potential passengers that they would ride with experienced pilots, who would be at the controls of safe planes. The Tourabout and another plane coming out of the NAC factory, the Speedster, were built especially for commercial and pleasure flying, according to the ad.

And the NAC's goal was more than getting a long line of paying airborne sightseers. The company wanted to sell planes. Readers were invited to make "a personal inspection of the aircraft industry." If someone took a demonstration flight, he or she would be persuaded to buy a plane, the NAC claimed.

The next step? Make a deal for a plane. Head to the Lincoln Flying Field on South 20th Street. Or stop by the office and factory at 12th and Q streets. Or call 133726.

An article that heralded Lincoln's growing prominence in aviation appeared in another Nebraska newspaper.

"Lincoln is Real Aircraft Center" was the headline of a report that said the MAC's Lincoln plant had become the third-largest airplane manufacturing and assembly plant in the United States., surpassed only by one run by Glenn Curtiss interests and a government plant in the east.

The NAC had been "completely reorganized" a few weeks earlier, and Ray Page had become the general manager. A reporter who toured the plant was shown more than a hundred airplane motors on hand plus enough parts to assemble forty or fifty planes.

NAC shipped three planes to Mexico City on August 15 of that year, bringing the total transferred to the country's air mail service to twelve aircraft. Apparently, the first nine planes were flown to points in Mexico for officials to test them, but they performed well enough that the government was willing to rely on testing done in Lincoln as satisfactory to accept delivery.

Page was termed a "former automobile man (who) is somewhat a crank on service." Page's philosophy was that an airplane owner was entitled to the same parts availability and service that the owner of a good automobile expected. Thus, Page maintained a "liberal supply" of parts, not only for NAC-manufactured planes but also for other popular makes.

That practice had resulted in a steady growth of the company's business, which was attracting planes from throughout Nebraska to be rebuilt or repaired. Consequently, Lincoln's importance as an aircraft center would continue to grow, Page said.

"Lincoln…has many advantages that no other town or city in the state has, and it doubtless will maintain its present position as the leading city west of the Mississippi river in the manufacture and distribution of aircraft," a newspaper report said.

A black cloud appeared on the horizon for NAC and Lincoln in May 1921. Gardner, a veteran flyer who had been an Army flight instructor, died of injuries he suffered when his plane crashed during an exhibition in Holdredge, Nebraska. The unmarried thirty-two-year-old pilot, who had family in in Joliet, Illinois, had lived in Lincoln and worked for the NAC for a year and a half.

The plane Gardner was flying at Holdredge was new and had been "carefully tested out." Gardner had been flying a while that day and had exhibited stunts that ended with a spiral.

Biffle, who accompanied Gardner to Holdredge, saw the accident. He said it was impossible to explain the cause. Gardner had pushed his plane into a long tailspin, and it appeared he was unable to pull the plane back up while just a few hundred feet from the ground.

Although Gardner broke no bones, he suffered head and neck injuries. He was partly conscious when he arrived in Lincoln on a Burlington Railroad train car.

"Gardner went into a tailspin at 1,200 feet and appeared at all times to have complete control of the ship," Biffle said. "It seemed to me that he tried to land from the spin as he was just in a good position to make a landing."

When friends reached the crash site, Gardner said to them, "Take me home. I am sick."

Biffle thought Gardner's forehead was crushed. The plane's throttle handle was broken, and Gardner's wrist was broken, which led Biffle to believe Gardner held the lever to the end.

Gardiner kept saying the plane was all right, and there was speculation that a strong southeast wind caught the plane's wing and caused Gardner to lose control as he tried to level the machine. By then, he was too close to the ground to avoid crashing.

Gardner had racked up ample experience in the still-new field of flight. He piloted the airplane that completed the first air mail run between New York City and Chicago. During World War I, he was a flight instructor at Kelly Field in Fort Worth, Love Field in Dallas, and at Chanute Field in Rantoul, Illinois. Aviation people considered Gardner one of the best fliers in the country.

When Lindbergh came to Lincoln less than a year later, Biffle was his flight instructor. Lindbergh undoubtedly heard about Gardner's crash. It's unknown if hearing about this fatality caused Lindbergh to reconsider flying as his life's path. It's likely, though, that Lindbergh, like others who flew in the 1920s, calculated the risks involved in piloting flimsy planes with imperfect engines and decided the reward of adventure made the potential danger something to be taken in stride.

By June 1922, when Lindbergh was finishing his flight lessons in Lincoln and making his first parachute jump, Page had purchased the NAC and was bullish on its prospects. The *Ace*, a leading aircraft publication, in an article reprinted in a Lincoln newspaper, spotlighted NAC, Page, and Lincoln's aircraft industry in its June 1922 issue, writing, "Business is booming in Lincoln, Nebraska and especially the aircraft business."

"The flying season is now open and each week finds new purchasers for Lincoln Standard airplanes in Lincoln. The Lincoln Standard airplanes are being put out on the market at a very attractive price, within the reach of all who are desirous of obtaining an airplane, and it can be used as a commercial commodity, rather than a luxury."

Page said NAC was attracting buyers who previously held off because they thought planes cost too much and their quality was too low. He touted NAC's planes as having "superior quality, durability and high efficiency." Lincoln Standard planes had a three-year track record of solid performance and could be bought in 1922 for "only" $2,950, the equivalent of about $52,000 a century later.

The *Ace* said Page was a strong aviation booster and "he is not leaving a stone unturned to prove the value of aircraft."

Page had developed "an excellent idea" to entertain Lincoln residents each weekend and to stimulate interest in aviation. That method was to hold exhibitions and stunt flying and other attractions "in keeping with the Game," as 1920s media called it, not only for locals but also for the benefit of visitors to the company facility.

"It looks as if aviation is going to be put on the map in Lincoln," the *Ace* said.

If Lindbergh read this and other flying-related pieces in what had temporarily become his hometown newspaper, it augured well for his future. The college dropout was getting positive reinforcement for his decision to seek his fortune in the sky. Barnstorming and a trip to Montana lay ahead.

TWO

Lindbergh's first flight

Lindbergh took his first flight as a passenger on April 9, 1922. He went into the sky in a Lincoln Standard plane piloted by veteran pilot Otto Timm, who had Montana ties. Timm came from North Dakota to Montana in the 1910s and flew exhibitions at Sidney and Harlowton during that decade. Lindbergh received his first flight lessons soon in the same plane soon after the April 1922 flight. His instructor was Biffle, who had a reputation at the Nebraska firm as the most hardboiled flight trainer the Army had during the just-ended Great War.

Lindbergh recalled spending the next two months in catch-as-catch-can flight instruction. He learned what he could around the factory because there was no ground school associated with the flying course then. The plan, not always followed, was to do most student flying in the early morning or as evening approached because strong Nebraska winds during the middle of the day created rough drafts that were challenging for a student pilot.

Yet Lindbergh said he got ample flight time in rough weather. That was because his instructor, nicknamed "Biff," had definite views on when to rise and shine. Biff believed early morning was not a proper time for flight instructors to awake, and because Biff was the only instructor and Lindbergh was his lone student , Lindbergh did little early morning flying and instead flew more later in the day.

By the end of May 1922, Lindbergh had logged about eight hours of instruction. He had spent $500 for the flying course and another $150 for train fare and personal expenses.

One day, Biff said Lindbergh was ready to make a solo flight. Ray Page, the president of the company, however, required a bond to cover possible damage to the plane. That was money Lindbergh didn't have, so he had to put off his first solo flight.

Before Lindbergh entirely finished his flying course, Page sold the student plane to E. O. Bahl, who planned to use it on a barnstorming trip through southeastern Nebraska. Lindbergh, who had met Bahl in Lincoln, offered to pay his own expenses if he was allowed to accompany Bahl as a mechanic and helper. This resulted in Lindbergh's going on a barnstorming tour through Nebraska towns southeast of Lincoln. Lindbergh credited Bahl with providing him his first experience in cross-country flight.

Flying with Bahl gave Lindbergh a deeper understanding of how airplane barnstorming worked. In 1922, typical barnstorming pilots, including Bahl, charged passengers five dollars for a ride of five to ten minutes; for most people in small farming towns, having a barnstormer fly overhead was the first time they had seen an airplane, and a brave minority became airborne for the first time.

While flying with Bahl, Lindbergh began wing walking. It seemed a good way to attract crowds (and potential passengers) to a pasture or stubble field that was the barnstormers' temporary base of operations. Bahl would fly low over the town while Lindbergh stood on a wingtip as onlookers gazed in awe.

During Lindbergh's time in Lincoln, he learned something else that would be valuable in the future: parachute jumping. Charlie Harden, a leader in parachuting in the booming aeronautical realm, arrived in Lincoln. Lindbergh had been fascinated by the parachute jumps he had seen, and he persuaded Page to let him make a double drop with Harden's chute.

Lindbergh said that a double drop involved two parachutes fastened with rope. To get the chutes ready, "both are then packed in a heavy canvas bag; the mouth of the bag is laced together and lace ends tied in a bow knot. The bag is lashed halfway out on the wing of the plane, with the laced end hanging down."

A parachute jumper rode with a plane until it reached a sufficient altitude, then the jumper climbed out of the cockpit and crept along the wing to the chute. He fastened the parachute straps to his harness and swung under the wing. This position held the jumper to the plane by the bow knot holding together the mouth of the bag containing his parachute. The bag was tightly tied to the wing.

When the jumper was ready to float toward earth, he pulled the bow knot, allowing the bag to open and the parachute to be pulled out by his weight. If done correctly, the first chute opened, after which the jumper cut the rope binding the two chutes. If all worked as planned, the first chute, no longer carrying the jumper's weight, would pass the other chute on the way down.

Lindbergh made his first jump, from 1,800 feet altitude, in June 1922 over the flying field, but the experience gave him pause. The first chute opened quickly, and Lindbergh floated downward a few seconds. He cut that chute from the original one, expecting the same sensation. But he didn't feel the tug of risers, which he had been told to expect in a jump.

"As I had never made a descent before, it did not occur to me that everything was not as it should be until several seconds had passed and I began to turn over and fall headfirst," he said, looking back five years after his rookie experience.

The jump turned out OK, though, when the harness jerked Lindbergh into an upright position. The chute opened, and he floated to the ground.

He later learned that the vent of the second chute had been tied to the first with grocery string. The string broke when the chute was packed so that the chute followed him, still folded, instead of billowing out.

That caused Lindbergh to free fall for several hundred feet before the primary chute opened, something that probably would have caused some, if not most, people making their first double parachute jump to reconsider making another jump. Lindbergh's thoughts at that moment aren't recorded, but he went on to use a parachute to bail out from planes with engine trouble several times as an air mail pilot in the years between his barnstorming trips and the 1927 trans-Atlantic flight.

By the summer of 1922, Lindbergh's ambition to participate in stunt flying and parachute jumping was solid. That goal, however, could have been squashed by an event in Chicago.

On July 2, 1922, Louis James, a wing walker and parachute jumper, was killed while trying to change planes over Homewood, a Chicago suburb. This fatality prompted the coroner's jury that investigated

James' death to recommend passage of legislation banning all forms of stunt flying.

"We believe that every accident is a great setback to aviation," read the jury verdict. "We do not want this to go on. It is well established that aviation is a necessity and should be encouraged. But we are all against stunt flying, wing walking and all forms of dangerous flying.

The verdict said James' death was accidental, and the other aviators who participated in the exhibition tried to avert the accident but had no chance.

"We therefore advise that immediate legislation be had to prevent all forms of stunt flying. There should be local, state, and national laws. Every pilot should be inspected. Every ship should be inspected. There should be no stunt flying."

James Curran, a veteran pilot flying the top plane in the maneuver, told the jury what he saw.

"We made three attempts," he said. "The last time I had decided the air was too rough for the stunt and was preparing to return to the field when I saw James reach for the ladder."

James, riding the top wing of the lower plane, grabbed the ladder, but a gust of wind hit Curran's plane and swung the ladder out, hurling James into the propeller of Curran's plane.

Roy Thompson, the pilot of the plane flying below Curran, testified, too, and his account matched Curran's. He said James, after being mangled in the propeller of Curran's plane, was thrown into the propeller of Thompson's plane. That impact shattered the plane's propeller and killed the engine, forcing him to land.

Ralph Diggins, owner of the planes, told the jury he was flying a third plane at the time and also experienced rough air.

An editorial in a New Jersey newspaper may have summed up public attitudes toward stunt flying as the Roaring Twenties drew to a close. "Let Aviation Curb Its Clowns" was the headline of commentary that mentioned an unusually high number of aviation deaths—whether in the area or across the United States, it's not clear. Fifteen people had died in a few weeks, including a stunt flier at Pine Valley.

"Some may take the attitude that if fools wish to rush in where angels fear to tread, even in airplanes, then why not let them pay a fool's penalty." That philosophy might work for reckless aviators, but it didn't help those who were more careful, the paper said.

The editorial declared that "little or nothing" was gained from stunt flying. If airplane manufacturers wanted to determine whether their machines could fly in "freakish positions," then have experienced pilots test them, in areas free of buildings and other obstructions, under authority.

"But allowing virtual novices to take up a plane and attempt all sorts of tricks, when they are scarcely capable of operating a plane in normal fashion, is simply inviting suicide."

New York's local flying fields had been the scenes of so many fatalities that there was talk of an official ban on stunt flying, something "that should not be necessary." Instead, clubs and organizations should clean up their own houses and block "stunters" from taking off from their fields. If stunt flying "abuse" continued, federal action might be merited. Yet, "we would regret to see any more prohibitory rules imposed when a little common sense and discretion would obviate the necessity for them."

By the time this editorial was published, it had been seven years since Lindbergh had thrilled— or frightened—spectators in Nebraska, Kansas, Colorado, Wyoming, and Montana with his wing walking. He had accomplished something far more risky—flying solo across the Atlantic—and he had married Anne Morrow. Together, they were flying the globe, scouting new air routes. Lindbergh's stunt flying days appeared to be over.

Proposals to ban stunt flying got publicity throughout the 1920s, and some local measures were adopted, but no national ban took effect.

THREE

Heading to Montana

Lindbergh stayed in Lincoln as the summer of 1922 approached, working in the factory to help manufacture Lincoln Standards for fifteen dollars a week. Then came the telegram that brought him to Montana. Lynch, a pilot originally from Ohio who had flown in the army in the Great War, had bought a Standard a few weeks earlier and taken it on a barnstorming trip into western Kansas. Now, he had contracts to perform flying exhibitions in Kansas and Colorado. He needed a parachute jumper and wired Lindbergh, asking if he wanted to join him under an arrangement that would have the young daredevil pay "a small fraction" of the trip costs.

Page offered Lindbergh a new Harden chute in lieu of his remaining flying lessons, and Lindbergh boarded a train bound for Bird City, Kansas, in the far northwestern corner of the state. Lynch and Lindbergh barnstormed over western Kansas and eastern Colorado for a while. Lindbergh usually made a parachute jump and did some wing walking.

Early on, Lynch, Bird City wheat farmer "Banty" Rogers, who had bought the plane, and Lindbergh stopped in the southeastern Colorado town of Lamar. Those who saw the appearance in early August 1922 were treated to the troupers' "specialty of theatrical stunts in the air." A local newspaper account seems to have gotten the act wrong, though, saying that it featured "Lynch taking a flying leap out of the plane while it is a mile high and going at a speed of one hundred miles an hour." It was actually Lindbergh who made the parachute jumps.

Lynch and company were headed to Monte Vista, Colorado, to perform at what was called a big celebration there. Then the barnstormers were expected to return to Lamar for another exhibition of stunt flying.

Another time, while Rogers, Lynch, and Lindbergh were barnstorming in Colorado, Lindbergh had a hair-raising experience. He thought he was a goner, so he decided to take a "selfie" of sorts, a picture of him using his aviation equipment, long before the twenty-first-century term came into vogue. This would be to help science if he died.

Lindbergh reasoned that people working to develop better parachutes would benefit from a photo of him taken seconds before his demise. The barnstormers were performing in the eastern Colorado town of Stratton when the incident occurred, according to Lynch.

Lindbergh's parachute didn't open, and he expected to be flung to death on the ground. Thinking fast, he pulled out his vest-pocket Kodak camera and snapped a picture of the half-open parachute above him as he whirled through space toward earth.

An instant later, he tugged the rope again. This time, the chute opened, and he landed safely.

"Slim got out on the wing that day and jumped off like he had a hundred times before," Lynch said in early September 1927, recalling the 1922 incident. Lynch said the blurry shot would show up as a smudge if reproduced in a newspaper.

Still, it triggered memories.

"He went down several hundred feet, and the ratlines wouldn't work. One side of the chute opened some, but the other was still collapsed. Slim worked himself out of trouble, though, and landed safely.

"The next day he showed me the picture. 'I thought it might be worth something to analyze chute troubles if I landed hard enough to finish me,' Slim told me."

Lindbergh's parachute obviously was a good one because he lived to finish the barnstorming tour and to go on to become an Army Air Service cadet and an air mail pilot and to fly solo across the Atlantic. Apparently, Lindbergh kept the grainy snapshot and showed it to people on his travels. Thus, a Kodak camera became a useful tool to the young flyer—something that would be verified a few days later when the barnstormers made an unscheduled stop on their way to Billings that turned into a memorable event.

After Lynch, Rogers, and Lindbergh crossed from Nebraska into eastern Wyoming, Lynch had to land once in Wyoming because of engine problems. The plane touched down near a herd of what Lindbergh said were buffalo (actually bison), and while Lynch worked on the plane, Lindbergh grabbed his camera, hoping to get a picture of the animals.

"I had not considered that they might object to being photographed, and was within a hundred yards of them when an old bull looked up and stamped his foot. In a moment they were all in line facing me with lowered heads," Lindbergh said. He snapped a picture and made a hasty retreat to the plane. By then, Lynch had finished troubleshooting, and the trio took off.

Lynch gave a later account of the encounter with the icons of the plains that was the same as Lindbergh's but more detailed.

Lynch said engine trouble forced him to land on

the prairie. As the plane dropped, he pointed out a herd of bison to his young passenger.

"While I was working on the ship, Slim went over a knoll looking for the buffalo. He was armed with a vest-pocket camera.

"Pretty soon, Slim came dashing up. 'The buffalo are after us,' he shouted. Sure enough, the buffalo came along. We had the plane in shape by then and hopped off," Lynch said.

The barnstormers then followed the Big Horn Mountains into Montana, where they flew over Custer's Battlefield, south of Hardin.

When Lynch, Rogers, and Lindbergh reached Billings in August 1922, there was lots of talk about flying. In fact, three individuals who would help shape Lindberg's aviation skills in Montana, Bob Westover, his brother, Ed Westover, and Todd Nelson, were at the center of local flying conversations at the time.

The buzz started when a plane operated by the Westover Standard Aircraft Corporation took off from Billings, bound for Wyoming's Big Horn mountains. Ed Westover and Nelson were supposed to leave at 6 a.m. but were delayed until just after 7 a.m. on a flight to deliver a special invitation to author Mary Roberts Rinehart to attend the Midland Empire Fair, which ran for four days in September that year in Billings.

Rinehart was one of the most popular novelists in America at the time. Often called the American Agatha Christie, she was spending the summer at the Eaton ranch in the heart of the Big Horn Mountains. The ranch, located at the mouth of Wolf Creek Canyon, was said to be "in as wild a district as has ever been reached by a flying machine."

The Westovers' Lincoln Standard plane, equipped

with a 150-horsepower motor, was expected to take two hours flying the 165 miles between Billings and the ranch in each direction. At Sheridan, Wyoming, the Billings aviators planned to pick up David Rowand, a young local businessman originally from Billings who would pilot the plane into the mountains.

Plans for the air journey started when the Westover company learned that the fair board planned to invite Rinehart to the fair, and company officials offered to deliver the invitation by air mail. James A. Shoemaker, manager of the fair, explained why Rinehart was a desired guest.

"The board of fair commissioners are particularly anxious to have Mrs. Rinehart with us at the coming fair since for the last seven years she has been an annual visitor in the West and is deeply interested in its development. Her experience and ability as a writer is recognized throughout the world, and more particularly is she especially gifted in the reportorial work, her last assignment having been the disarmament conference at Washington," he said.

Shoemaker said Billings officials had been told that Rinehart had experienced health problems for several months as she recovered from a major operation. Still, they hoped she would be able to come to the fair as a community guest. Her presence "will mean much to all our people, who are already well acquainted with her through her many writings." Shoemaker added a personal invitation to Rinehart to attend the September 19-22, 1922, fair. He said commissioners and area residents hoped she would accept so they would "have an opportunity of entertaining you in a truly western spirit."

He described Nelson and Westover as experienced mountain pilots who had volunteered to fly the invitation to Rinehart and await her answer. They were doing "their bit toward bringing about a greater Midland Empire Fair," and the same spirit of cooperation among Billings area residents made the fair "a superior exhibition."

Westover and Nelson, after leaving Billings an hour later than they planned, bucked a headwind that slowed them down. While crossing the Crow Reservation, they chased a band of wild horses led by a pinto stallion for several miles.

After picking up Rowand in Sheridan, they flew toward the Eaton ranch, twenty miles west in the Big Horn mountains. They circled at a high altitude, looking for a landing place, and finally saw a cavalcade on horseback in a meadow about a mile from the ranch and landed there.

With fanfare, Rinehart said yes to Billings' invitation. She wrote her acceptance "in a picturesque meadow of the Eaton ranch in the Big Horn mountains with 100 mounted guests of the ranch as spectators."

It took just a half-hour of conversation with the Billings men, after the Westover plane landed, for her to decide she would go to the fair. She told Shoemaker that the plane made a "superb landing" on the mountain meadow, where she sat while writing the message. She said she expected to remain in the West through September and that she would attend the fair if her plans didn't change.

FOUR

Treasure State thrills

In *We*, Lindbergh said he, Lynch, and Rogers took off in the fall of 1922 for Montana. This is at odds with accounts of Billings people (published in the *Gazette*), who recalled Lindbergh's arrival in the city as a barnstormer in the summer of that year. Also, an ad in the *Gazette* on August 22 trumpeted the upcoming appearance by Lynch, Lindbergh, and Booster, the dog that came along, at the Hogan Aviation Field, three miles west of Billings on the Laurel road. Furthermore, the barnstormers performed in Hardin, forty-five miles southeast of Billings, five days in August before their scheduled August 27 exhibition in Billings.

In Lindbergh's defense, he wrote *We* (actually rewrote it because he wasn't satisfied with the first version penned by a ghost writer) in a matter of weeks shortly after his trans-Atlantic flight.

We may have been the first of the so-called instant books, accounts of events that had just happened, that are designed to capture readers because of their timeliness. Compounding matters, Lindbergh had instantly become the most famous person in the world, and the press, celebrities, and politicians all wanted his time and attention. A twenty-five-year-old man, shy by nature as Lindbergh was, should be excused for less-than-perfect attention to details of a barnstorming trip that had happened five years earlier.

Lindbergh's first performance in the Treasure

State was in Hardin, the Big Horn County seat, located ten miles north of the Custer Battlefield, as it was then known.

People in Hardin may have wondered who they saw later, because the local newspaper misspelled Lindbergh's name and gave Rogers an incorrect nickname in describing the entourage's performance.

"Accompanying (Lynch) are General Manager 'Soak' Rogers, Mechanic Chas. Lindberger and 'Booster,' an English fox terrier which has the distinction of being the only dog known that rides on top of the plane, not only on straight flights, but during stunts and trick flying."

Lindbergh/Lindberger was labeled "an aerial acrobat and parachute man." Readers were told that Lynch, an Ohio native who served in the Great War, was an instructor and airplane tester at McCook Field in Field in Dayton, Ohio, and at "Chinook" Field in Rantoul, Illinois (actually Chanute Field). Before the war, Lynch worked in the Glenn Martin airplane factory in Cleveland, according to the Hardin Tribune.

"He has been handling planes for the past ten years, during which time he has taken up thousands of passengers, the oldest of whom was a man 94 years of age and the youngest, a pair of twins two weeks old."

Several Hardin residents mustered the courage to climb aboard Lynch's plane and see their town from the air. The locals who flew included the youngest and oldest Hardinites to ever fly at that time, eighty-eight-year-old A. C. Henderson, and five-year-old Bernadine Miller.

Lynch, Lindbergh, and Rogers left Hardin on Saturday morning, August 26, 1922, reportedly headed for the West Coast by way of the Montana cities of Billings, Butte, and Helena.

Lindbergh was so unknown when he came to Montana that summer that not only the *Hardin Tribune* but also the *Billings Gazette* misspelled his name—badly—in an article about the barnstormers who were coming to town.

The *Gazette* article, headlined "Aviator to Do Parachute Jump," said the parachutist would leap from his plane at a 3,000-foot altitude. Prospective passengers were promised flights of fifteen and twenty minutes during the Billings show. They would get to see, in the words of the Gazette, "H. L. Lindbourg," who was the parachute jumper and wing walker. Adding to the flair of the show, the entourage included Booster, their dog, who rode "turtleback" on top of the plane during its stunt flights.

No record exists of Lindbergh's reaction to having his name misspelled at least three times by Montana newspapers in 1922. The twenty-year-old, however, must have sensed that high adventure awaited him in Montana.

Commercial aviation was in its infancy then, leaving barnstormers with almost no choices for a solid career as a pilot, so they eked out a living by taking curious—and brave—spectators at impromptu air shows up for brief flights.

Lynch gave an example of the hand-to-mouth existence of barnstormers based on what happened to Lindbergh when they were in Colorado, heading toward Montana, in 1922.

"One day I went to Denver and gave 'Slim' fare to Limon (Colorado) and a few dollars above expenses, for money was pretty tight with us then. Anyway, I was delayed in Denver for several days, and when I arrived in Limon, Slim was flat broke and getting ready to make a loan on a pair of shoes."

When Lynch told that anecdote in early September 1927, Lindbergh was nearing the halfway point of his so-called "Goodwill Tour," having stopped in Boise and preparing to fly to Butte. By then, Lindbergh was reported to have turned down deals that would have brought him seven million dollars. His fame had vaulted him to presidency of the first airline planning to fly passengers along northern U.S. routes. The airline planned to launch service between St. Paul and Seattle, a trip that would take eighteen hours.

But when Lindbergh, Rogers, and Lynch set out on their 1922 barnstorming tour, an affluent, 1920s, Great Gatsby-like lifestyle was still a distant dream for Lindbergh. He and his companions patterned their performances in ways similar to what other barnstormers used to attract paying customers: for maybe ten dollars, people could get into the passenger seat of a flimsy biplane for a fifteen- or thirty-minute sightseeing flight over their town. Barnstormers would often start a show with acrobatic flights and other derring-do, including wing walking. Then they would land, hoping that their routine would bring enough paying traffic to buy a meal and put enough gasoline in their tanks to fly to the next town. Lodging for barnstormers often entailed sleeping under the wings of their planes, parked on a farmer's land that served as an airfield, with the moon and stars as the roof over the roamers on balmy late spring and summer nights.

Lynch used this approach to hustle business in Billings and took out a newspaper ad that read: "Free.

See It With your own eyes. A Thrilling Parachute Jump from a flying plane at 90 miles an hour—never seen before in Billings."

The enticement to watch the exhibition included a picture of a biplane in flight, beneath which readers were introduced to "Aerial Daredevil Lindberg (sic) with Pilot Lynch and their pet dog who's (sic) stunt is spectacular Aerial Flying."

The ad said Lynch and Lindbergh would land at the Hogan Aviation Field, which was then farmland three miles west of the Billings city limits on the road to Laurel. (Today, that early airstrip is paved over, part of Homestead Business Park, and businesses such as Costco, Fuddruckers and Outback Steakhouse stand where Lynch and Lindbergh once landed and took off.)

After Lynch and Lindbergh had been in Billings about a week, Lynch traded planes with O.L. "Shorty" Reese, a pilot who was flying a Lincoln Standard that belonged to Lloyd Lamb of Billings. Lynch and Lindbergh stayed in Montana while Rogers returned to Kansas.

Lindbergh barnstormed in Montana and northern Wyoming until mid-October 1922. His and Lynch's major performances took place at the Midland Empire Fair in Billings in September and at the Central Montana Fair in Lewistown.

Bob Westover recalled a near-death experience that his young employee experienced while in Montana. Lindbergh was earning a "modest" living as a parachute jumper advertising Westover's garage on First Avenue North in Billings, Westover said.

Lindbergh went about fifty miles from Billings one Sunday to show his skills at Red Lodge. He leaped from a plane with a string about the size of a fish line attached to his parachute. The string was supposed to straighten out the parachute, cause it to open and snap under Lindbergh's weight.

But the string failed to break. That left Lindbergh dangling a few thousand feet in the air. He faced the prospect of a fatal fall to the ground, crushed by the plane when it hit the ground. Unfazed, however, Lindbergh untied the parachute from his waist, pulled himself to the top of the parachute, climbed the string and crawled out on the rope.

He pulled up the parachute, cut the string, tied on a lighter one and jumped successfully.

Westover, who got to know Lindbergh during the four months he lived in Billings in 1922, said the Minnesota youngster made a strong impression on him as he performed parachute exhibitions throughout the area

"Slim was the quickest guy to leave a ship I ever saw," Westover said five years later. "He was gone before the pilot knew it. He seemed to jump out of an airplane as easily as he would step out of an automobile."

Lynch and Lindbergh didn't always find success with their Billings flying and wing walking exhibitions. On one Sunday afternoon in late August 1922, for example, they performed at the Hogan field in a show that drew this newspaper headline: "Aviators Give Thrills, Crowd Proves Air Shy."

The event attracted a big crowd, a reported 5,000 people, a quarter of Billings' population at the time. About 200 cars that lined the edge of the field, but "the aviating troupe secured few passengers." Instead, spectators were content to see "H. L. Lindbergh," another erroneous name used again by the *Gazette*, make a "spectacular and successful drop from the parachute from an attitude of several thousand feet." Lindbergh's parachute carried him about a half mile west of the field, where he landed in open country.

Once again, Booster got newspaper ink.

"The English terrier, one of the party, rode in the cockpit while the plane was making the loops as well as in plain sailing," readers were told.

FIVE

Flying at the fairs

The Midland Empire Fair opened, and Lynch and Lindbergh's aerial skills were overshadowed by a more Western tradition on opening day. "Broncho Fury Tries to Kill Unhorsed Man" read a headline, with a subhead that said races and bucking contests were the star features of the fair's opening day when "Billings Folks Flock to Grounds in Thousands" with September sunshine "smiling" on them.

Lynch and Lindbergh had made several exhibitions in and around Billings by the time the Midland Empire Fair started. One might have thought their scheduled appearance at the fair would draw a good deal of publicity, but it didn't.

When the fair ended on September 22, 1922, it was banner-headline news in the *Gazette*: "From Babies To Beef. Montana's Best Fill Stage On Final Day." The seventh annual Midland Empire Fair drew a record 55,398 attendees, including 14,786 on Friday, the closing day.

"Everyone was turning homeward Friday night, satisfied with the splendid exhibition and with the magnificent way in which it has been brought to the fore as, more than ever, Montana's greatest fair."

Yet, the Lincoln barnstormers rated only passing newspaper mention and that in anonymous fashion.

"The airplane exhibition was particularly good, Friday, several loop-the-loops and nose dips being successfully accomplished," read a one-sentence summary buried deep in the article.

It wasn't until July 1927 that a more detailed account of the Lynch-Lindbergh exhibition at the fair in Billings surfaced. Here's what Lindbergh wrote in his first-person account of his life, from childhood through the trans-Atlantic flight:

"At Billings ... our field was some distance from the fair and we decided to devise some scheme to bring the crowd out to us. We stuffed a dummy with straw and enough mud to give it sufficient falling speed to look like a human being.

"When the grandstands were packed that afternoon we took off from our field with the dummy in the front cockpit with me. I went out on the wing and we did a few stunts over the fairgrounds to get everyone's attention, then Lynch turned the plane so that no one could see me on the wing and we threw out the dummy. It fell waving its arms and legs around wildly and landed near the Yellowstone River."

Lynch and Lindbergh returned to the Hogan field and waited expectantly for a throng of people who wanted to go up for a flight. Two hours later, "a few Montanans did arrive," but they offered a different version of what had happened from what Lynch and Lindbergh had hoped for.

"[T]hey told us about one of the other attractions—a fellow who dived from an airplane into the Yellowstone River which was about three feet deep at that point."

That was the last time the barnstormers tried to thrill a Montana crowd, Lindbergh said.

In 1931, four years after Lindbergh was hailed as an all-conquering hero when he stopped in Butte and Helena, and Montanans everywhere cheered him, *Billings Gazette* readers got Bob Westover's version of the

Midland Empire fair "dummy" event, almost identical to Lindbergh's tale but with more detail.

Westover said Lindbergh and Lynch thought crowds would rush to the Hogan field to get gruesome details about the "man" who fell into the river, but the handful of people who showed up seemed wise to the prank. They said they had seen what appeared to be a man dive from the plane into the river, but that didn't make sense because the river was in low flow and only about three feet deep at that point. Westover said Lindbergh came up with the idea, which succeeded better than he thought—several women spectators were badly upset by the staged mishap.

Westover said a stunt like that—if presented in 1931—would get a pilot in hot water with the U.S. Department of Commerce, which regulated aviation then.

Memories of Lindbergh's 1922 sojourn in Billings persist to this day among descendants of people who interacted with him. One was Billings resident Phil Scala, whose grandfather started Billings Cabinet Company, which did all kinds of woodwork, in 1912. C. A. Warner, the shop owner and Scala's grandfather, told of a young pilot who came into the shop one day and asked if it could repair the wooden propeller of his airplane. Warner didn't know who the flyer was, but he turned out to be Charles Lindbergh. The shop repaired the propeller, and Lindbergh was pleased.

"My grandfather was always very proud of that job," Scala said a century later.

Not everyone in Billings held fond memories of Lindbergh's 1922 stay in the city. Local historian Joyce M. Jensen said Lindbergh was a hero to most in the city, "but to at least one Billings businessman, he simply was one who skipped town without paying his bill. Frank Spencer owned a restaurant on Montana Avenue where 'Slim' sometimes ate. He always charged his food.

"Then he left town without paying. Spencer was the kind who never would have dreamed of sending Lindbergh a bill, so Spencer never did think too highly of Lindbergh."

Jensen, elaborating in 2022, said Spencer became part of her family sometime in the second decade of the twentieth century. Her grandfather, Nathaniel Martin, and his brother, Ben, taking advantage of bumper cucumber crops in the Huntley Irrigation Project, started a pickling plant there. In 1915, Martin moved the plant into Billings, locating it along Moore Lane.

Frank Spencer apparently ran away from an abusive family situation in Massachusetts. He came to Billings, went to work at the Martins' pickling plant, and became friends with Jensen's father, Robert "Bob" Martin. Spencer was considered part of the Martin family, Jensen said. Sometime in the early 1920s, Spencer either opened or became associated with a restaurant on Montana Avenue. The exact address is unknown, but it likely was close to the Westover garage on the 2300 block of First Avenue North, making it convenient for Lindbergh to drop in for a meal.

After Lindbergh's fabled New York-to-Paris flight, "Frank never contacted him," according to what her father told her, Jensen said.

Lindbergh left one other memory with the Martins and others who knew him during his time in Billings. Jensen said Lindbergh was sometimes addressed as "dirty neck Slim" due to his habit of wiping his hot and sweaty hands on his neck.

After Lindbergh and Lynch finished performing at the Midland Empire Fair in Billings in September 1922, they took off for Lewistown. There, attendees of the Central Montana Fair were treated to aerobatics similar to those Billings spectators had seen.

Here's Lindbergh's description of what happened in Lewistown:

"At the Lewistown fair, we obtained a field adjoining the fairgrounds and did a rushing business for three days. We had arranged for the fence to be opened to the grounds and for a gateman to give return tickets to anyone who wished to ride in the plane. All this in return for a free parachute drop."

Lindbergh's use of the phrase "rushing business" is backed by a newspaper account of that year's fair. "Perfect weather" helped the fair draw a crowd of about 8,000 people to the Friday-night closing session. The fair finale was described as the best of the week, complete with "uniformly good" races and other features that were "exceptionally entertaining." People came from Harlowton and other central Montana points, and they helped the fair set what was then an attendance record.

It was not, however, the first time that people in Lewistown and central Montana were treated to airborne antics. Two years earlier, they saw another pioneer pilot, who was from Montana, dash through the sky overhead. And in a quirk of fate, this flier also flew a few times with Charles Lindbergh, thus bonding them in the close-knit fraternity of early fliers.

The trailblazing pilot who flew in Lewistown and nearby towns in 1920 was someone whom later generations of Montanans got to know as a perennial, gadfly candidate for U.S. president who lived in Phillipsburg.

Long before that, though, Merrill Riddick was one of the best-known pilots in the United States during the time immediately after the Great War ended in 1918. Riddick, born in 1895, was a son of Carl Riddick, who represented Montana's eastern congressional district from 1919 to 1923. The younger Riddick joined the Army Air Service in the war and became a flying instructor.

Born in Madison, Wisconsin, Merrill Riddick came to Montana at about age eleven. His father was a typesetter who moved his wife and four children to a homestead near Lewistown in 1906.

Soon after the November 1918 Armistice, Riddick etched his own name in flying history. In the summer of 1919, he began flying the Washington-New York mail route, and a year later, he set a record for the trip with a time of one hour and fifty-five minutes.

A Rochester, N.Y., newspaper account said Riddick left the Army Air Service (then responsible for air mail) to "satisfy his wanderlust." And that's how he crossed paths with Charles Lindbergh, who had not yet attained global fame.

In his 1979 newspaper interview, Riddick reminisced about reportedly landing the second contract to fly air mail in the country. His deal with the government called for him to fly between New Orleans and Pilot Town, on the mouth of the Mississippi River.

Although Riddick had a "bunch of surplus planes," he didn't have the capital to make the business successful, so he couldn't "keep up" and "failed miserably."

His saga continued.

"In a fit of despair, I went across the river where I had an old airplane tied to a fence in Beaumont, Texas.

I tried to fly it and landed in some tall grass in a Texas town and couldn't take off," he said.

Someone traded him an old car, missing a dashboard, for the plane, and Riddick drove to St. Louis.

"Lindbergh was up there, and the Robinson brothers, and they financed me on a modern plane," Riddick said. He apparently made a mistaken reference to the Robertson brothers, Frank and William, wartime fliers who had started their own air mail company, according to Berg's biography of Lindbergh. Their company, Robertson Aircraft Corporation, was awarded the second Contract Air Mail route, called CAM-2, between Chicago and St. Louis in October 1925. As described in Chapter 10, Riddick likely crossed paths with Lindbergh in St. Louis in July 1925.

SIX

Boating the Yellowstone River

By October 1922, the Montana fair season was over and barnstorming opportunities had dried up. It was time for Lindbergh to return to Lincoln and resume training to become a pilot.

But for a twenty-year-old man with a yen for adventure, taking the train from Billings to Nebraska evidently seemed a ho-hum idea. Lindbergh hatched up a scheme that seemed more in the spirit of William Clark, who had canoed with his men down the Yellowstone River on the Lewis and Clark Expedition's return trip from the Pacific Coast in 1806. Or perhaps he got inspiration from reading Mark Twain's story of Huck Finn's voyages on the Mississippi River.

Lindbergh bought a small boat in Billings for two dollars after returning from the Lewistown fair. He patched it, which stopped the larger leaks, then set off alone on the Yellowstone, headed for Lincoln.

"The river was not deep and ran over numerous rapids which were so shallow that even the flat bottom of my small boat would bump over the rocks from time to time," Lindbergh wrote.

"I had been unable to purchase a thoroughly seagoing vessel for two dollars, and very little rough going was required to knock out the resin from the cracks and open the old leaks again."

Lindbergh had lashed his camping equipment atop one of the boat seats to keep it dry. As he floated downstream, over rocks and through rapids, he spent more and more of his time bailing out the boat with a tin can. He traveled about twenty miles the first day but clearing water from the boat took up half of the time he spent on the water.

Lindbergh camped on his first night out in a clearing beside the river. He pitched his army tent on dry ground, ate a cold supper, and crawled inside the blankets he had sewn together to make a bag. It was a cold—and likely miserable—night because showers during the day that had soaked the ground turned into steady rain after dark.

When morning came, the sky was still overcast, but the rain had stopped. Lindbergh ate a quick breakfast, packed his gear in the boat, and set off again.

The rain came back, and Lindbergh's boat was leaking even worse as rocks took a toll on the sides and bottom of the makeshift craft. He was bailing water almost constantly, and rowing the boat was of no use or need. By evening, Lindbergh's boat was beyond repair.

The aspiring flier decided that river travel was no longer possible, and that's when he crossed paths with farm boys who lived east of Billings.

As recounted almost forty years later, a fourteen-year-old boy encountered Lindbergh that day, but the youth had no idea who he had met until years later. The boy, E.W. Kraske, whose family farmed in the Huntley Irrigation Project east of Billings, was walking through a pasture surrounded by yellowing cottonwoods to herd cows in for their nightly milking. The youth's chores were interrupted, as described in a 1961 *Gazette* article: "Suddenly (he) stopped. Looking down towards the river, he saw a man standing up in a small boat."

Kraske watched, fascinated, as the man—Lindbergh—rowed his boat through fast water and disappeared behind a bank.

About an hour later, Kraske was pumping water at a well when Lindbergh appeared. Dressed in doughboy trousers, high-top leather boots and a slip-on sweater, he was carrying a large, white earthen water jug.

Kraske said the stranger asked him how far it was to Custer, a town downstream on the Yellowstone River at the eastern edge of Yellowstone County, and "he was quite surprised to hear that it was about 35 or 40 miles."

The farm boy pumped Lindbergh's jug full of water, and the adventurer returned to the woods along the river, where he made a camp for the night.

"After supper my two brothers Emil and Paul, both younger than I, went with me to see how our visitor was making out. Mother warned us that he might be a convict or someone on the run from the law, but this didn't stop us. We were curious and excited about having a camper on our place," Kraske said.

"His camp was about a quarter mile from the house on a high bank next to the river. He had an Army pup tent set up with a sleeping bag in it. He had a campfire going. Several pairs of heavy woolen socks were drying on sticks set up near the fire. We stayed and talked a couple hours and then went home."

The next day was Saturday, so the Kraske boys didn't have to go to school. They spent nearly the entire day with their new friend, whom they found to be "very good company."

Still-a-stranger Lindbergh told the youths he had left Billings two days earlier. It had taken him two days to float and row to a point a little northeast of Worden.

He had slept the previous night in an abandoned cabin along the river, which gave him dry quarters instead of being in the rain and sleeping in his tent on wet ground. Adding to his troubles, Lindbergh had overturned his boat in a shallow riffle, soaking all his bedding and supplies. But he was able to save all his camping items, according to Kraske.

"His groceries at the time he camped at our place consisted of a few potatoes, a package of pancake flour and several cans of beans and peaches."

Lindbergh's cooking utensils included a frying pan, a few tin cups, and a couple of pots. The stranger showed the Kraskes a small pan in the boat, which contained oakum, hemp rope fibers for caulking boat seams, and a few nails. It was obvious that the boat was in poor shape and needed repairs. Lindbergh told about buying the boat in Billings.

"It leaked badly and kept him busy bailing and rowing. I don't blame him a bit for giving up his idea" of going all the way to Lincoln in the boat, Kraske said.

The next day, Sunday, the Kraskes had dinner guests, the Pallas family, which included three cousins of the boys. Seven kids, four Kraskes and three Pallases, trooped down to the river to see Lindbergh.

When the youths got to the camp, the would-be voyager asked Kraske and his brothers if they could help him get a ride to Worden. He had decided to abandon the idea of floating down the Yellowstone and Missouri rivers to St. Louis. The Kraskes said they'd ask their parents to arrange a ride for Lindbergh, almost certain that the customary hospitality towards strangers would prompt the favor to be given.

The young man from Minnesota and his new

Montana friends sat around the campfire for a while. Lindbergh opened a few cans of peaches and shared them with the youngsters in cups, cans, or whatever containers were on hand.

Lindbergh was short of spoons, so he showed the improvisational skills that would come in handy later. He fashioned extra spoons out of pieces of willow with his jackknife.

Lindbergh broke camp, taking down his tent, rolling up his sleeping bag and throwing a few cans of food and his frying pan into the bag. He placed the bag inside his tent and tied the oars to the side of the boat, ending with a compact pack. Lindbergh gave the water jug and remaining food to the Kraskes and Pallases. The eight young people slogged to the Kraske farmhouse, where E.W.'s mother was making dinner. She invited Lindbergh to join them for a meal.

"He gladly accepted," Kraske said.

After dinner, the Kraskes hitched a horse to their buggy—they did not have a car then—and set off on a forty-five-minute trip to Worden. They arrived in time to catch the local train, called the "Dinky," which arrived at about 1:30 a.m. and took riders west into Billings.

When Lindbergh got to Billings, he waited a bit at its bustling train depot on Montana Avenue, where more than two dozen passenger trains arrived and departed daily. People could choose from among the Northern Pacific, Burlington, and Great Northern railroads to travel north, south, east, or west across the United States. He probably caught a Burlington train to Lincoln.

(The 1909-vintage depot still stands. It was rescued from possible demolition in the 1990s and, as part of the Billings Historic District, is used for weddings, business functions and other events.)

"As far as I can remember, he never told us his name or asked what ours was," Kraske said. He guessed that Lindbergh was nineteen years old at the time; he was actually twenty. The youths did learn their visitor was from Minnesota.

"None of us knew who he was until late in 1927 or early in 1928 when my brother read the book, *We*, which Lindbergh wrote a few months after his New York-to-Paris flight.

"In it, our camper related the experience of trading a boat for a wagon ride to town.

"Just think—it was only a few years before his famous flight that Charles A. Lindbergh camped at our farm and ate dinner with us!

"Lindy is one visitor I'll never forget."

SEVEN

A plane of his own

After accepting the hospitality of the Kraske family, Lindbergh was on his way back to Lincoln, Nebraska. When he got off the train at the state capital, his first task was to repair his motorcycle. Just before he had left Lincoln the previous summer, he'd raced a car with his motorcycle along a country road and jammed a piston on the bike. He spent a few days fixing the piston, then took off to visit his mother, Evangeline, in Detroit.

It took him three days to get there, and he spent about two weeks in Michigan before he was on the go again. He boarded a train for Little Falls, Minnesota, to take care of business on the family farm. He spent part of the winter months of 1923 on the acreage and part in Minneapolis with his lawyer-congressman father. Sometimes, they would drive together to Little Falls, 100 miles away. He also took a train to Florida, where his father owned real estate.

Lindbergh never lost sight of what had become his lifetime goal. As he recalled, he'd had an ambition to own an airplane ever since he got in the air for the first time in Lincoln in 1922.

"So, when I took my last flight with Lynch in Montana and started down the Yellowstone, I had decided that the next spring I would be flying my own ship."

To further that goal, in April 1923 Lindbergh left Miami and set off for Americus, Georgia, an Army base during the Great War that was being shut down. Americus was one of the places where the federal government was storing war surplus Curtiss JN-4 planes, trainers nicknamed "Jennies." Lindbergh bought one, equipped with a new Curtiss Ex-5 motor, for $500, a fraction of its original price tag. Thousands of Jennies were sitting at airfields across the country, awaiting either new owners via auction or disposal by being crushed as junk metal. Lindbergh missed the real bargain days at Americus; the year before, some Jennies had been auctioned for as little as fifty dollars.

A few days after Lindbergh got to Americus, the last officer left his post, and it became one of the "phantom airports" that were a vestige of the war. Most Americans first became aware of the town in the mid-1970s when Jimmy Carter, an Americus native, successfully ran for president.

Lindbergh lived alone on the Army post in Americus while his plane was being assembled. He slept in either one of the remaining hangars or one of the barracks buildings, vestiges of the days when the post was part of U.S. war efforts.

His connection to Montana was renewed one day when the pilot with whom Lynch had traded planes in Billings flew in. Reese stepped out, and the two exchanged stories about their 1922 experiences.

Lindbergh noted the camaraderie among aviators.

"One of the interesting facts bearing on the life of aviators is they rarely lose track of one another permanently. Distance means little to the pilot, and there is always someone dropping in from somewhere who knows all the various flyers in his section of the country, and who is willing to sit down and do a little 'ground flying' with the local pilots," Lindbergh wrote. ("Ground flying" meant the exchange of flying experiences by pilots.) This allowed "intimate contact" to continuously exist among what Lindbergh called the "clan" of fliers.

Lindbergh had not soloed in a plane when he bought his Jenny, but he and his former colleagues in Lincoln were among the few who knew. At Lincoln, he got a taste of flying with Bahl and Lynch, but he wasn't allowed to solo there. Thus, when Lindbergh's Jenny was ready to fly in Americus, he was unsure of what to do. Not only had he never soloed, he hadn't been in a plane for six months, and he didn't have money to pay for more flight instruction. He decided to try flying alone.

He got in his Jenny, opened the throttle, and started to take off. His plane rose only four feet off the ground before the right wing began to drop, so Lindbergh landed. He skidded to a stop on one wheel, but fortunately didn't damage the Jenny. He noticed that the wind was blowing considerably and decided he would return to the hangar and wait for calmer conditions.

Apparently, Lindbergh's lack of flying time, as a pilot and not as a wing walker and parachute jumper passenger, and its effect on his flying ability caught the eye of another pilot who was in Americus to pick up another Jenny. This more experienced aviator offered to give Lindbergh dual instruction. They flew together for thirty minutes and made several landings.

The touch-and-go sessions prompted the other pilot to tell Lindbergh that he would have no trouble flying and was just rusty from lack of airtime. The individual advised Lindbergh to wait until evening to make a few solo flights in calmer air.

That evening, after making a final instrument check, Lindbergh completed his first solo flight. He described it as one of the events in a pilot's life that are permanently etched in the pilot's memory.

"It is the culmination of difficult hours of instruction, hard weeks of training and often years of anticipation. To be absolutely alone for the first time in the cockpit of a plane hundreds of feet above the ground is an experience never to be forgotten."

Lindbergh flew practice flights from Southern Field for a week, then he was off on another adventure. He rolled his equipment and spare parts in a blanket, lashed them in his Jenny's cockpit, and took off for Minnesota on his first cross-country flight.

Less than a week after his first solo flight, and with barely five hours of solo flight time under his belt, Lindbergh was flying cross country alone. He did, however, have the advantage of "invaluable experience" gained in 1922 while flying in Montana and other western states with Biffle, Bahl, and Lynch.

When Lindbergh left for Americus in April 1923, he wrote his father, promising to let him know the results of his search for a plane he could buy. During that same period, he was writing to Chambers of Commerce, offering flying exhibitions for $150 a day. He imagined giving shows that included parachute jumping, wing walking and airplane stunts at local fairs. He was set to put on shows.

It had been only about nine months since Lindbergh packed his newly acquired parachute and began barnstorming, the adventure that brought him to Billings, Lewistown, and neighboring Montana towns and hamlets. Now, in the spring of 1923, flying his own Jenny, he was becoming a more polished pilot every day.

Lindbergh wrote that while learning to fly in Lincoln, the word from other airmen was that most pilots had flown in Texas sometime during their careers. Following their example, he included the Lone Star State in his route from Georgia to Minnesota, although Texarkana was the only Texas city he planned to fly into.

He said he crossed "rough territory" while flying from Americus to Montgomery, Alabama, but he had been warned that the real challenge was navigating over "some of the worst flying in the south" in Texas. Conventional wisdom said that he should follow a northern course directly to Minnesota or follow the Gulf of Mexico. That line of thinking, however, created a challenge in Lindbergh's mind. He wanted to see what the "worst flying country" was like.

"I had a great deal of confidence in my Jenny with its powerful OX-5 engine, and it seemed absurd to me at that time to detour," he said, so he planned a route in the most direct line possible, considering the Jenny's limited cruising range based on its forty-gallon fuel tank.

After an uneventful flight to Montgomery, Lindbergh landed at the Army field there and filled his tank. He continued his odyssey, making stops in Meridian, Mississippi, and a rural location halfway between Maben and Mathison, Mississippi. There, he experienced his first crackup when, after landing in a field, he decided to taxi toward the fence corner to better take cover from an approaching storm. Faster than he could react, however, the landing gear plunged into a ditch. The propeller hit the ground, and the tail of the Jenny rose skyward and turned almost completely over before coming to rest at a forty-five-degree angle.

Fortunately, only the propeller was damaged in the accident, although the wings and fuselage were covered with mud. Local people helped Lindbergh lift his plane out of the ditch, and he wired a contact at Americus to have one of two propellers he had purchased there before leaving shipped to him. Lindbergh got a room at a local hotel and, once the propeller arrived and he had swapped it with the broken one, found lively business taking local residents up for plane rides at five dollars per person. He stayed in Maben two weeks and took more than sixty passengers for rides, raking in $300.

People swarmed to Lindbergh's plane from the surrounding country; some traveled fifteen miles in ox carts to see the Jenny fly. Using language acceptable to many people in all parts of the country at the time, Lindbergh, in *We*, recalled one Black woman who approached him and asked: "Boss! How much you all charge foah take me up to Heaben and leave me dah?"

Lindbergh said he could have taken more passengers, but constant rain left the ground so wet that each flight rutted the field badly. He needed help—men pushing on the wings—each time the plane rolled over a soft spot that was on his takeoff route.

Lindbergh searched for but was unable to find another suitable field for his flying purposes. That obstacle helped inspire him to the insight that was to motivate him throughout his aviation career—that flight, to be commercially viable, required dedicated, well-maintained landing fields. That is, true airports.

"Landing fields are of primary importance to safety in aviation," he wrote. "It is not a question of how small a field an plane can operate from, but rather of how large a field is necessary to make that operation safe."

Cities needed to develop large, well-equipped airports close by to foster the growth of commercial airlines. That would do much to keep the United States at the forefront of aviation activity. That theme—the need for U.S. superiority in aviation—would mature in Lindbergh's mind, leading to his trip to Nazi Germany in the 1930s to check out Adolf Hitler and Herman Goering's drive to build the Luftwaffe, Germany's air force. This occurred first in secret, then openly, in defiance of the Versailles Treaty enacted after Germany's defeat in the Great War and of other agreements achieved during the disarmament movement of the 1920s.

Lindbergh's flight to Minnesota was the start of his air odyssey. In the next few weeks, he flew over Georgia, Alabama, Mississippi, Texas, Louisiana, the Ozark mountains, and Kansas before he eventually reached Lincoln.

In Lincoln, Lindbergh rejoined Bud Gurney, the young fellow flier who had gone up with him in Otto Timm's plane on a first flight for both Lindbergh and Gurney. This time, Gurney wanted to test a parachute he had made. His plan was to get up to an altitude of 1,500 to 2,000 feet and jump from the plane. He'd be successful if the chute opened.

Lindbergh talked Gurney into using Lindbergh's Jenny for the test flight. The first test would be made with the added weight of a sandbag. His gas tanks full, Lindbergh took off with the parachute and sandbag lashed to the right wing. Bud, who weighed 165 pounds, got into the cockpit, and the Jenny took off with a total load of about 600 pounds. Additional resistance came from the parachute and sandbag, which sat in the propeller's slipstream; still, the Jenny took off and cleared the nearest obstacle safely.

The plane climbed to about 200 feet, then it was buffeted by a downdraft that dropped it to seventy feet off the ground. Lindbergh couldn't get any higher, and ahead of him loomed a wooded hill. He turned downwind to avoid striking trees, then he had to clear a railroad trestle, which he did by inches. He motioned for Gurney to cut the sandbag loose, but when Gurney climbed out of the cockpit, he created more resistance. The plane dropped lower, and ahead of Lindbergh were trees he knew he couldn't clear.

Lindbergh saw a grain field below him. He cut power and landed downwind in grain tall enough to keep the Jenny from rolling. Lindbergh and Gurney unloaded the sandbag and had no trouble taking off and flying back to the airstrip. Gurney later successfully tested his parachute, and the two young adventurers took off on their own barnstorming trip through eastern Nebraska.

Other barnstormers had beaten them to the turf, so they had little business. The trip did, however, give them experience in surviving the electricity, lightning, and the heavy rain of a violent thunderstorm. The two had had to sit out the storm before flying on. Once in Lincoln, they slept on the field, Lindbergh in a hammock and Gurney in the back of a Ford truck.

EIGHT

Flying with father

Lindbergh flew on to Shakopee, Minnesota, where he planned to help his father, a former congressman, campaign to reach Washington again by flying him around Minnesota. This area is where Lindbergh experienced his first true plane crash. It happened after he found Shakopee socked in by rain and detoured to the nearby town of Savage.

One of his Jenny's cylinders cut out, and Lindbergh started circling, hoping to land in a clover field. He was less than 200 feet in the air and losing altitude, so he had to land at once. His only option for a landing places was a spot between a swamp and high trees. He aimed for the swamp. He cut the throttle, and when the wheels touched earth, they rolled twenty feet and sank, and the plane nosed over.

The mishap took no more than three minutes to play out. When it ended, Lindbergh was hanging onto the safety belt. When he tried to open the clasp with one hand—he was using his other hand to hold on to the body of the plane and keep from falling out—he found the clasp to be jammed. He had to undo two strap buckles to get out of the cockpit.

Lindbergh inspected his plane and found little serious damage. The propeller was cracked and would need to be replaced, and there was a crack in the spreader board that he repaired with strong cord. The plane was splashed with mud but otherwise in good condition.

Lindbergh walked through the swamp to the nearest farmhouse. As he went, he noticed solid ground along the edge of the swamp less than 100 yards from the plane that he could use to take off.

The occupant of the farmhouse near the swamp had seen Lindbergh's plane fly over in the rain. He met Lindbergh and told him he couldn't get his horses through the muck out to the plane to pull it out.

Lindbergh borrowed a rope from the farmer and used it to pull the plane's tail back to a normal position. While this was going on, two boys alerted the Savage townspeople of the accident. They had seen Lindbergh land, and when he was delayed in getting out of the cockpit, they ran to town and told passersby that a plane had landed upside down in the swamp. The boys claimed they had felt the flier's neck, found it stiff, and thought him to be dead.

Soon, the swamp was swarming with townspeople. They converged on the plane so that by the time Lindbergh and the farmer arrived, there were enough people to help lift the plane back onto solid ground.

The June 1923 incident gained notice in one of the Minneapolis newspapers. In an article headlined "Lindbergh Airplane Breaks Propeller in 200-foot dive," the paper reported that Lindbergh was waiting for a new propeller to arrive from his hometown of Little Falls, Minnesota, so he could resume helping his father vie for a seat as United States senator from Minnesota, replacing the previous senator, Knute Nelson, who had died in office. The senior Lindbergh ran in the special election on the Farmer-Labor Party ticket.

Having survived nights when he slept in a hammock he made from canvas and hung under a plane wing, along with heavy rain, floods, high winds, primitive airports and emergency landings, Lindbergh rendezvoused with his father in Marshall, Minnesota.

Lindbergh wanted to show his father how an airplane would allow him to blanket a town with campaign flyers. C. A., as the senior Lindbergh was known, got in the plane armed with hundreds of handbills. Charles told him to throw the paper out when he rocked the plane and nodded. Charles said what happened:

"It did not occur to me that he might throw them out all at once, but he did, and the thick stack of sheets struck the stabilizer with a thud."

C.A. would have been the first Minnesota senator from the Farmer-Labor Party if he had been elected, but he lost, finishing third.

Lindbergh spent the rest of the summer of 1923 barnstorming-in Minnesota, Iowa, and Wisconsin. He was usually alone although he had a student join him and learn to fly while he was performing.

Some weeks, Lindbergh barely covered his expenses, and other weeks, he was busy taking passengers up at five dollars each. Overall, he made a modest profit after paying for his expenses and depreciating the Jenny.

NINE

The break he needed

One evening in the summer of 1923 while Lindbergh was waiting for "chance" passengers at an airstrip in southern Minnesota, he experienced a light-bulb moment. A car drove up, and in it were several young men, including a graduate of the Army Air Service Training Schools.

This person suggested that Lindbergh apply to enlist as a cadet at Brooks Field in San Antonio. The procedure was to write to the Air Service chief at the War Department in Washington and ask for enrollment forms and program information, Lindbergh learned. He was immediately interested because he had wanted to fly modern, powerful airplanes for some time. While at the Lincoln flying school, he saw fourteen DeHavilands with 400-horsepower Liberty engines fly in, a sight that kindled his desire to fly the planes.

The Army, of which the Air Service was part, offered Lindbergh his only chance to fly a Liberty-engine-equipped plane because none were being used for barnstorming. So that night at his hotel, he wrote the Air Service chief, and a few days later he received a reply, including an enrollment form. The letter said a candidate had to be between 20 and 27 years old, unmarried, in good physical condition, with a high school education or its equivalent.

Lindbergh completed the forms, mailed them back to Washington and soon received another letter. It instructed him to appear before an examining board at Chanute Field in Rantoul, Illinois, in January 1924.

This gave Lindbergh time for more barnstorming. He began heading south because cold weather in Minnesota made most people uninterested in flying in an open cockpit. He veered into Wisconsin but found that the market had been figuratively spoiled by another barnstormer who had carried passengers for half-price. Lindbergh said he followed the informal rule of the time, which was "giving a good ride for five dollars but not carrying anyone for less."

With little or no business to be had in Wisconsin, Lindbergh pointed his plane toward Illinois. He flew over the state and headed towards St. Louis, where the International Air show was in progress. As he flew toward St. Louis, a low gas tank forced him to land. He filled up from a passing gas truck and flew toward Carlinville, Illinois, where he refueled again and picked up a St. Louis-bound passenger, who paid twenty-five dollars for the flight.

As Lindbergh and his passenger approached St. Louis' Lambert Field, they saw the bombers contest going on. He landed on a hill east of the field and waited until evening to move his plane to the end of a long row of civilian aircraft.

The air show allowed Lindbergh to reunite with old friends, including Gurney, who had come from Lincoln with another flying school student. Gurney had brought his parachute and was entered in the parachute spot-landing contest. He was scheduled to be the last performer of the meet, when he would exhibit a double drop.

In the evening, after taking up a handful of passengers, Lindbergh checked out the planes that had flown in. He later said he would have gladly traded his meager profits from that summer's barnstorming for a chance to fly some of the newer plane models he saw in St. Louis. Nothing would stop him from being appointed an Army flying cadet, he vowed.

"This appeared to be my only opportunity to fly planes which would roar up into the sky when they were pointed in that direction instead of having to be wished up over low trees at the end of the field," he said.

Fulfilling his promise to take Gurney up for his last jump of the show, Lindbergh helped his Lincoln buddy tie two chutes together with an old rope, the only one they could find. The two wondered about the reliability of the rope but decided it would hold and cause a longer fall before the second chute opened.

Lindbergh "wished" his aging Jenny up to 1,700 feet and cut Gurney loose. The first chute opened immediately, but the strain on the rope was too much. It snapped, releasing the second chute. Gurney fell another 300 feet before the chute opened. That left Gurney falling through air filled with planes flying everywhere, none seeming to be aware of the Lindbergh-Gurney team. Turbulent air stirred by propellers caused Gurney's chute to swing back and forth, and he landed with a thud on the side of a ditch. He broke an arm as a result, the only injury accident during the show, according to Lindbergh.

Lindbergh had planned to keep on barnstorming, heading south after the St. Louis show, but he changed his mind and sold his Jenny to a friend of Gurney's. Lindbergh took on two flying students, one learning on the Jenny he had just bought from Lindbergh, the other a student of another pilot who had flown in from Minneapolis with a plane that he sold in St. Louis. This pilot needed to return home, and his student needed a new instructor.

Lindbergh taught his students air skills, made a quick barnstorming tour in Illinois, and flew his old Jenny to his main student's home in Iowa. After watching the student make some solo flights near his home, Lindbergh got on the train to Lincoln. He had told his student to keep a "safe gliding angle" over the city when flying and to always stay at least 1,500 feet in the air. His last sight of the old Jenny was of it flying 300 feet over the train station in the center of town.

Now a true itinerant flier, Lindbergh was traveling to Lincoln to pick up an SVA, a two-seat Italian pursuit plane supposedly sitting there. But when he arrived, he was told the plane was parked in a field in Omaha and that cows had eaten all the fabric off the rudder.

Lindbergh had to get inventive. He and a companion filled a car with a new rudder and spare parts and drove to Omaha, where they found the plane in even worse condition than had been represented. Not only did it need a new rudder, but the fabric in the wings was also loose because of broken stitching. The radiator leaked, and someone had tried to fix that by pouring in a pail of bran. When Lindbergh finally got the engine running. it skipped and wouldn't rev beyond 1,100 rpm.

Still, Lindbergh decided to try to fly the plane to Lincoln where, using the experience he had gained as a mechanic in Billings, he could better work on the machine. Five minutes into the air, the plane was almost boiling over, the temperature gauge showing 115 degrees. In fifteen minutes, the water tank exploded.

Lindbergh landed in a stubble field. He hired a farmer to hitch his team of horses to the plane and haul it to a corner next to his house. Lindbergh left the plane to be taken apart and trucked to Lincoln.

December 1923 found Lindbergh barnstorming in Illinois. "Some weeks, I barely made expenses, and others I carried passengers all week long at five dollars each," he said. Lindbergh made a "fair profit" after accounting for expenses and depreciation while in this phase of barnstorming as a pilot and no longer as a wing walker and parachute jumper.

With the nomad phase of Lindbergh's life winding down, in January 1924 he went to Chanute Field in downstate Illinois to take his examinations to become a flying cadet.

Serious flying was still a ways off. Lindbergh wouldn't know until he reported to Brooks Field in March whether he had been accepted into the next cadet class. So, he and Leon Klink, a car dealer who had bought a Canuck (the Canadian version of the Jenny), took off into the Ozarks for what became Lindbergh's final barnstorming trip. Klink wanted to learn to fly and take a vacation while Lindbergh wanted to keep his flying skills sharp, so the pair settled on a pleasure flight; they barnstormed only enough to pay their expenses, if possible.

On January 23, 1924, Lindbergh and Klink left St. Louis' Lambert Field in five-below weather, their plane pointed toward warmer places. They visited towns such as Perryville, Missouri, and Hickman, Kentucky; made a refueling stop in Tennessee; and landed in a cotton field at Friar Point, Mississippi, where they tied down for the night.

Flying a Canuck imposed severe limits on a pilot's range. The plane had a twenty-three--gallon fuel tank, enough to last for two and a half hours of flying. A pilot needed to allow a half-hour of flight time to find a field for landing. That meant the plane could fly about 135 miles in still air, less if it was bucking a headwind.

A few months later, in early 1924, Lindbergh found out he been accepted as a cadet and began his training as an Army pilot at Brooks Field in San Antonio. He received sad news from Minnesota in May of that year. His father had died from an inoperable tumor while making a final political campaign, this time for governor. He was sixty-five.

Lindbergh could not get immediate leave, so in accordance with his father's wishes to have his body cremated, Lindbergh disposed of the ashes during a flight over the Lindbergh family homestead in Melrose, Minnesota, that fall.

The senior Lindbergh was in a coma for several weeks after surgery at the Mayo Hospital in Rochester, Minnesota, on his deep-seated brain tumor. The efforts didn't succeed, and he spent his final days in St. Vincent's Hospital in Crookston, Minnesota, where he could be close to his daughter, and Charles Augustus Lindbergh's half-sister, Mrs. G. W. Christie, of Red Lake Falls, Minnesota, who was at his bedside when death came.

Lindbergh returned to Texas and resumed his Army flight training. He survived the so-called "Benzine Board," a practice designed to weed out as many cadets as possible. He was among nineteen of the 104 cadets who started flight training who were still on the rolls a year later. He graduated first overall in his class in March 1925, earning his Army pilot's wings and a commission as a second lieutenant in the Air Service Reserve Corps.

Lindbergh's most serious flying accident occurred

on March 5, 1925, eight days before graduation, when he was involved in a midair collision with another Army S.E.5 plane during aerial combat maneuvers. He bailed out and wasn't injured.

Lindbergh traced his development as a focused, goal-oriented individual and an aviator to the year of military training he had completed. The Army didn't need more active-duty pilots then, so after graduation, Lindbergh again worked in civilian aviation as a barnstormer and flight instructor. He did, however, get a chance to continue part-time military flying after he joined the 110th Observation Squadron, 35th Division of the Missouri Nation Guard. He was promoted to first lieutenant on December 7, 1925, and to captain in July 1926.

His father had been initially opposed to Lindbergh's notion of flying, but his mother was a different story. Evangeline never objected to her son's aviation inclination, so after meeting him in Janesville, Minnesota, and getting her first airplane ride, she became a flying enthusiast. Evangeline made several barnstorming flights with Charles before his 1927 flight, and she was a passenger on one of her son's round-trip air mail flights between Chicago and St, Louis, riding in the plane's mail compartment.

TEN

Flying the mail

By 1925, Lindbergh had become well-known enough to draw attention from the one of the newspapers in St. Louis, the city that would help boost him to global fame. The *St. Louis Globe-Democrat* ran an article with the headline "Hair-Raising Stunts Planned For Aerial Program Saturday." It said fliers with national and international reputations would be on hand for the July 1925 exhibition, among them Lindbergh, by then a lieutenant in the Army on reserve status. Readers were told that he was the only man in the country who had escaped a midair collision with another plane, a reference to Lindbergh's accident in Texas earlier that year.

"He is a widely known stunt flyer and will put a plane through the loops while Manley Merrell, an aerial performer, stands upright on top of the airplane," the newspaper reported. Also on hand was Montanan Merrill Riddick, labeled an "aerial hobo," who lived then in Owensboro, Kentucky.

Then, in late June 1925, Lindbergh nearly duplicated his near-death Army feat at Bridgeton, Missouri, where he was living after his discharge from the army. Lindbergh was 3,000 feet in the air when his plane started to fail. He released his parachute several hundred feet in the sky and floated safely to earth.

When 1926 began, Lindbergh became involved in the branch of flying that would bring him a level of fame exceeded only by his trans-Atlantic flight. He became an air mail pilot, hired by the Robertson Aircraft

Corporation (RAC) at Lambert-St. Louis Flying Field, where he had been working as a flight instructor. RAC assigned him to lay out and serve as chief pilot for a brand-new, 278-mile contract air mail route between St. Louis and Chicago, with intermediate stops in the Illinois cities of Springfield and Peoria.

Lindbergh and three other RAC pilots, Phillip R. Love, Thomas P. Nelson, and "Bud" Gurney, Lindbergh's friend from their Lincoln days, flew mail in four modified war-surplus de Havilland DH-4 biplanes.

On April 13, 1926, Lindbergh took the United States Post Office Department's Oath of Mail messengers, and he opened service on the route two days later. Soon, the air mail got a boost toward profitability. Congress passed a bill providing for payment to air mail contractors on a poundage basis instead of by percentage payment for each package carried. That purportedly resulted in a reduction of letters that needed to be carried daily, from 5,000 to 2,500, on the St. Louis-Chicago route for it to be in the black.

Still, Maj. William Robertson, contractor for the route, said more air mail usage would be needed to make the service a paying proposition. It didn't take long for that to happen.

Lindbergh flew the first air mail flight from Chicago to St. Louis on April 15, 1926. He arrived at Lambert Field at 9:07 a.m., eight minutes ahead of schedule. The two pouches of mail got to the main post office at 10 a.m. and were delivered during the forenoon.

Lindbergh left Maywood Field in Chicago at 5:50 a.m., a few minutes after the East Coast plane arrived. It had no mail for him to carry, but he picked up a St. Louis-bound sack of mail at Peoria as well as one going to Springfield. At Springfield, he picked up another mail sack for delivery to St. Louis. His flying time for the 265-mile run was two hours, thirty minutes. He was running ahead of schedule and had to wait twenty-five minutes in Peoria.

Springfield and Peoria were approaching their expected amount of mail daily, Robertson said. The new rate schedule required 185 pounds of mail daily, about 2,500 pieces, for profitability, and the daily letter count ranged from 1,100 to 1,300 during the first six weeks that the route operated. Since the April 15 start date, about 49,000 air mail letters had been sent from St. Louis, Robertson said.

Banks, wholesale and retail mercantile companies, and electrical companies, early adopters of air mail, had come to count on its reliability. They valued the time saved in getting mail to Chicago and then on to New York City and other Eastern seaboard destinations. Letters mailed in St. Louis and intended to catch the afternoon plane to Chicago reached there in time to be put on planes to New York for delivery in that city the next morning. Likewise, businesses that got mail on the afternoon plane out of New York could expect to have it reach St. Louis the following morning.

Robertson was proud of the record compiled by the three mail planes of his company at that early date. They had logged forty-three round trips between St. Louis and Chicago and traveled 25,800 miles without an accident. The Chicago-New York connection had been missed once, when a storm forced a pilot to make an unscheduled landing in Streator, Illinois.

Excellent equipment and capable pilots made possible the exemplary record, Robertson said. He singled out Lindbergh's flying ability, highlighted in a recent event. The mail from New York arrived at Chicago's

Maywood Field in a severe rainstorm. Lindbergh loaded the St. Louis mail in his plane and took off immediately while other pilots waited for the storm to subside. Lindbergh arrived in St. Louis on schedule.

Lindbergh's flying legend grew in September 1926 when he survived a daring parachute jump while carrying mail. Fog blanketed the countryside near Chicago, forcing him to fly for hours above the fog bank that brought down three air mail planes before his descent.

His plane running out of fuel, Lindbergh grabbed his parachute and jumped while nearly a mile high above Wedron, Illinois. His pilotless plane crashed, but the mail still got through. Lindbergh reportedly walked two miles to the wreck site after touching down, pulled three pouches of mail from the plane, and arranged to have that carried the final sixty miles to Chicago. Lindbergh bailed from his plane after cruising for more than two hours above the Chicago air mail terminal. People there directed powerful search lights skyward, trying to pierce the fog. They heard the drone of Lindbergh's plane engine and grew increasingly concerned about his delayed arrival before word of his rough but injury-free landing reached them.

The fuel in his plane dropped so low that Lindbergh, who had circled westward to Ottawa, Illinois, had to open his emergency gasoline tank. He said his altimeter read 5,000 feet when he saw the emergency tank reach a completely empty state. Still hidden in the fog, he realized he would have to "go over the side"— that is, jump by parachute from a doomed plane, for the third time in his flying experience. Lindbergh dropped through a fog blanket that he estimated to be 1,000 feet thick and landed without a mishap.

During the early part of his descent, however, he

was constantly in danger of being hit by his plane. It whirled about, its wings coming within a few hundred feet of Lindbergh at times.

Lindbergh had company in his ability to escape a plane safely when confronted by bad weather. The first air mail plane forced down by fog was on the national air transport route from Dallas. Its pilot landed at Rock Falls, Illinois. An hour later, another mail plane touched down at Spring Valley, Illinois. Finally, pilot Jack Milatzo flew 160 miles from Bryan, Ohio, to Chicago in an hour, only to find his destination hidden by fog. He retraced his route back to Bryan and landed with less than a half-gallon of gas in his tank.

Less than two months after the September 1926 bailout, Lindbergh survived his fourth parachute jump from a plane that was no longer flyable. On November 3, 1926, after leaving St. Louis for Chicago at 4:15 p.m., he found himself flying in darkness, with snow and sleet whipping around him at 13,000 feet with the plane engine dead. He dove headfirst over the side of his plane after a failed three-hour search for a landing place, which emptied his fuel tank.

He dropped more than two miles and landed uninjured on a barbed wire fence six miles west of Bloomington, Illinois. The never-say-die pilot got on a train to Chicago. From there, he flew another plane back to Bloomington to look for the wreckage of his original plane and three pouches of mail it was carrying.

More accolades came Lindbergh's way as 1927 started. On January 14, he completed the first night air mail flight from Chicago to St. Louis, guided by new lights along the route. He arrived at Lambert Field at twelve-fifty a.m., after a flight of two hours and fifteen minutes. Lindbergh made the night flight so that he would have ample time to pilot the return air mail flight back to Chicago.

Lindbergh left Maywood Field at 10:35 p.m. As he flew southwest, his route was illuminated by twenty-four revolving electric beacons. Strung about ten miles apart from Chicago to St. Louis, they were installed at a cost of $80,000. Lindbergh's employer, the Robertson Corporation, got the contract to install the lights.

It was at that time that Lindbergh gained 1920s-style fame as the champion civilian parachute jumper. For example, the newspaper in the Montana city where he lived for three months as a barnstorming wing walker published an article declaring Lindbergh the country's champion parachute jumper as a member of the "Caterpillar Club." This organization was made up of "aviators whose lives have been saved by a flimsy bit of silk."

The article recounted the times that Lindbergh, his plane disabled in the sky or out of gas, relied on his chute to get back to the ground, starting with his March 1925 jump out of a plane involved in a midair collision at Kelly Field in Texas. He never suffered a serious injury in any of the four jumps he made.

Although Billings would come to claim Lindbergh as one of its own, the *Gazette* article made no mention of his time in the Magic City.

ELEVEN

The Atlantic beckons

By mid-February 1927, Lindbergh's time as an air mail pilot was over. He left the Midwest for San Diego to oversee design and construction of the plane that would take him across the Atlantic, the *Spirit of St. Louis*.

Lindbergh and others were drawn to competition for the Orteig Prize. This $25,000 award was put up by Raymond Orteig, a French-born New York hotelier who first offered the money in 1919 to whoever made the first successful nonstop trans-Atlantic flight between New York and Paris. The flight could be in either direction.

Orteig originally specified that the prize winner had to complete the 3,600-mile flight within five years of when he dangled the money before aviators—that is, by 1924. When that deadline passed without a successful flight, Orteig extended the prize window for another five years.

This time, several well-financed fliers, all better known than Lindbergh, came forward to compete. All tried but all either failed or flew across the Atlantic after Lindbergh captured the Orteig Prize and world adulation.

First, Great War French flying ace Rene Fonck left New York's Roosevelt Field on September 21, 1926. His Sikorsky S-35 crashed on takeoff. Two crew members were killed, but Fonck survived,

Next, U.S. Naval aviators Noel Davis and Stanton H. Wooster died at Langley Field, in Virginia, on April

26, 1927, while testing their Keystone Pathfinder. Perhaps the most famous unsuccessful attempt occurred just days before Lindbergh took off. French war heroes Charles Nungesser and Francis Coli left Paris' Le Borquet Airport on May 8, 1927; they were piloting a Levasseur PL 8 seaplane nicknamed L'Oiseau Blanc. The two disappeared somewhere in the Atlantic after last being seen crossing the west coast of Ireland. To this day, no sign of them or their plane has been found.

American air racer Clarence D, Chamberlain and Bert Acosta crossed the Atlantic and flew to Germany in mid-June 1927. Finally, Arctic explorer Richard E. Byrd flew to France in late June 1927 and ditched on the French coast.

By May 20, 1927, when Lindbergh took off from Roosevelt Field, heading for Paris, the whole world was waiting and watching. The multitude of well-wishers included his former boss in Billings.

"I thought of him a lot. I guess I called up (to the *Gazette* office) about every hour when he was making the trip across (the Atlantic) until I learned that he was safe," Bob Westover said.

By then, Westover had sold the plane from which Lindbergh made parachute jumps in Billings to a Helena man. A photo in the Gazette showed Nelson and Westover with this 150-horsepower training plane. The day after Westover sold the plane, the new owner broke one end of the propeller. Westover got back the propeller, described as an "old type spoonbill affair," and hoped to use it in a clock. He changed his mind after Lindbergh crossed the Atlantic and kept the propeller as a memento of the now-famous Minnesotan's time in Billings.

Blanket coverage of Lindbergh's feat included a

reminder for residents of Billings and nearby towns of Lindbergh's brush with death during a 1922 appearance in Red Lodge. In the spring of 1927, seemingly all Billings was abuzz with the news, and residents were bringing forth memories of the "Slim" they had met as an unknown wing walker five years earlier.

Commenting on Lindbergh's work as a mechanic, Westover said his employee was a very thorough mechanic and a good employee. Lindbergh also helped keep Westover's plane working and had a good knowledge of its parts.

Westover recalled that the barnstormers took up a collection when they showed up for a parachute jump and stunt flying. They weren't successful pied pipers, however; the small number of fares from "hopping" passengers meant the plane did little more than cover expenses. Lindbergh thus left Billings with little more money than when he came.

In his non-flying time, Lindbergh usually could be found at the garage. When he had nothing to do, he sat on the running board of a car or in a corner with nothing to say, according to Westover. Lindbergh was known among the men who worked at the garage as a "clean-cut fellow," Westover said. The young flier had no bad habits: no partying, no smoking, no ingratiating himself with his peers.

"He was respected, however, and we all knew that he had plenty of guts. The boys liked him in spite of his quiet ways."

Whenever Lindbergh got ready for a jump, he packed his own chute and made sure everything was right. He was confident that his parachute would open and acted on that confidence. His planning and confidence served him well on his solo flight from New York to Paris, Westover said.

"He displayed exactly the same spirit when he figured out with so much gas, so much power, and so much weight what the *Spirit of St. Louis* ought to do on the flight across the Atlantic. Then he went ahead expecting to do it."

Maybe the rest of the world called Lindbergh "Lucky Lindy," But to everyone he knew in Billings, he was "Slim." He signed letters to his Billings friends by that moniker, even after his Atlantic flight gave him global fame.

From October 1922, when Lindbergh left Billings, until about three years later, Westover didn't hear from his adventuresome former employee. Then Lindbergh wrote to Westover, giving him an account of the 1925 midair collision he survived with another Army flier while the two were practicing a formation attack.

Westover got one other letter from Lindbergh before the 1927 flight that changed his life for good. Westover shared memories of when he and Lindbergh teamed up, Westover piloting his Lincoln Standard plane for exhibitions that featured Lindbergh's wing walking and parachute jumping at Red Lodge, Cody, Winnett, Roundup, Rapelje, Molt, and other towns near Billings. Memories floated through the air of Lindbergh's jumps in Billings, most of them at the Hogan airstrip. People were pleased to remember or hear for the first time that Lindbergh never had any accidents during those shows.

Another memory came from George F. Shea, manager of the Northern Hotel, who was a passenger with Lynch and Nelson while Lindbergh was in Billings. Shea said Lindbergh had a narrow escape on his first Billings jump. His parachute carried him close to the smokestack of the Great Western Sugar Company on Billings' South side, and Lindbergh landed on a lumber pile behind the factory.

Shea recalled another time, an afternoon when he flew with Lynch in Westover's plane. Shea planned to take a boat trip down the Yellowstone and wanted to scout the river. The men were late getting back, and it was getting dark when they reached the airstrip. Lindbergh, who had built a bonfire and used it to guide them in, was waiting when they landed.

Early-day Billings farmer Ben Hogan, whose land was the airfield from which the Nebraska barnstormers took off and landed, also got to know Lindbergh and chimed in after the 1927 flight with incidents involving him that occurred in 1922. Hogan said Lindbergh, while quiet and taciturn, still played pranks that showed he had a sense of humor. For example, a group of girls gathered around the plane and leaned on a wing. Lindbergh got into the cockpit, started the "booster" and probably smiled when vibrations from the machine shook the girls off the plane. Another time, Hogan's son, Benny, was touching the plane. Lindbergh asked him to pick up a monkey wrench, and when he did, Lindbergh started the booster and gave the boy a shock.

An event in neighboring Laurel brought out Lindbergh's playful side. After Lynch, Lindbergh, and Hogan flew to Laurel, Hogan said he had to get back to his farm to milk the cows, so the trio returned to rural west Billings. They returned to Laurel that night in Hogan's car. The festivities included a wrestling match in which well-known wrestler Jake Amend (for whom Billings' Amend Park is named) was one of the contestants. Lindbergh parked Hogan's car four or five feet from the stand where the wrestling match was taking place, but the crowd packed in to watch the match kept Hogan and Lindbergh from seeing it. Lindbergh took the wheel and by "twisting and juggling" the car maneuvered it right up to the stand, crowding spectators out of the way.

Lindbergh's bashfulness around girls meant they couldn't get a word out of him, according to Hogan. Once while Lindbergh was folding his parachute, he ran out of papers that he placed between each fold. Hogan said he had a bunch of newspapers in his farmhouse and came back with a pile of old copies of the Gazette. As Lindbergh methodically placed the papers between each fold of his chute, several girls crowded around him and began teasing him.

"What are you going to do, Slim, advertise the *Billings Gazette*?" they said, trying to rattle him. Lindbergh said nothing. He kept on putting papers in the folds, never looking up. When he jumped, he scattered newspapers all over the field.

Another memory of the 1922 barnstorming trip to Billings involved Booster, Rogers' fox terrier. The small dog loved to fly and always rode on the plane, kept in place with a harness locked to the platform from which Lindbergh jumped. Lindbergh took care of the dog. Once, one of the pilots who flew the Lincoln Standard forgot to bring Booster on board for a flight. The dog jumped on the platform when the plane started and managed to keep his footing in the air. The dog apparently showed his annoyance at the pilot by biting him in the neck. On another occasion, after a pilot went through several stunts that didn't seem to get the dog's approval, he nipped the pilot on the neck.

It was common for a thousand or two thousand spectators to show up to watch Lynch and Lindbergh's performance, Hogan said. Few, though, were brave enough to go up in the plane. They needed assurance that flying was safe, so Lynch would take Hogan and his wife up for a ride. That seemed to allay the fears of some prospective passengers, and it was a good deal for the Hogans, who got several free airplane rides by helping Lynch coax customers.

Several times while Lindbergh was in Billings, the Hogan family had him at their home for a meal. The Hogans got used to his "diffident nature," which made him the butt of jokes. Yet, the Hogans grew fond of Lindbergh's youthful nature and inexperience in life.

"He was a good boy," Hogan said.

Although Lindbergh never flew a plane while he was in Billings—his first solo flight was about seven months after he left Montana to go back to Lincoln—several Billings people mistakenly claimed later that Lindbergh took them up for sightseeing flights.

Lindbergh traveled light when he came to Billings in 1922, bringing only a toothbrush and a pair of goggles that he carried in his khaki coveralls, his only clothing outfit. He shared a room at the El Niblo Hotel paid for by Ed Westover, with a third occupant being a man employed at the Westover garage. Later, the trio moved to the Harvard Hotel, where they again shared a room. Lindbergh slept on the floor on warm nights, "and at other times, they made out three in a bed," as the *Gazette* put it.

A decade after his trans-Atlantic flight, Lindbergh shared another memory of his time in Billings. He recalled working for the Westovers as a night attendant, "sitting up in the dusty garage office, playing an old phonograph to pass the time, selling gasoline to an occasional traveler in the dark. I can still remember some of the words of one of the records I played during those nights: 'In the quaint old town of Richmond, of Civil Wartime fame, there lived a Southern maiden, Virginia was her name.' "

For years after he met Lindbergh, Westover kept as a memento a miniature airplane that Lindbergh helped build and part of the propeller from the plane that carried Lindbergh into the sky. In the fall of 1927, Westover started a flying school in his Billings garage. For the first lesson, attended by seven students, he used the model plane to illustrate flying principles.

TWELVE

Taking Butte by storm

When Lindbergh returned to Montana in September 1927 during his cross-country tour of all forty-eight states, it would have been hard for many of the Treasure State's slightly more than half a million residents not to have heard he was coming. Some of the newspapers that heralded his appearance at the state fair in Helena (its site before it moved to Great Falls) included the *Hardin Tribune*, the *Sanders County Independent*, Kalispell's *Flathead Courier*, the *Mineral Independent*, the *Townsend Star*, and the *Dillon Tribune*.

The *Dillon Examiner*, another paper in the Beaverhead County seat, carried a half-page ad on September 7, 1927. It depicted Lindbergh's Ryan plane flying across the mountains juxtaposed with an eagle perched on the logo for Sunburst Refining, an early facility serving Montana's growing petroleum industry. The ad said it was a "mark of distinction" to have the Great Falls company, manufacturer of "Powerized" gasoline, chosen to provide the gasoline Lindbergh would use while flying at the state fair.

Also, the company touted its role as supplier of gasoline for other fliers who would participate in the air meet at the 1927 state fair, which ran September 5-9.

The *Choteau Acantha* published an ad on August 25, 1927, for Lindbergh's appearance at the fair. It consisted almost entirely of a picture of him in his flight jacket and headgear.

Butte, which got to roll out the red carpet first, was set to host spectators coming from every part of Montana and from neighboring states who would make up "one of the most cosmopolitan gatherings that the flying colonel has ever addressed." All was set as the Mining City, called "The Greatest Hill on Earth" for its enormous deposits of copper that wired America for the age of electricity, eagerly awaited the arrival of "The Lone Eagle."

Two Montana railroads got in the promotion act. The Northern Pacific Railroad, which ran between Butte and other cities and towns west of the Continental Divide (as well as east to Bozeman, over Bozeman Pass to Livingston, then along the Yellowstone River valley to North Dakota and Minnesota) offered a special five-dollar round-trip rate for passengers traveling from Missoula to Helena, where the state fair was underway and where Lindbergh would fly after his Butte appearance. A few days earlier, the Great Northern Railroad offered a cent-a-mile rate for travel on its line within a radius of Butte or Helena.

The stir caused by Lindbergh's impending arrival spread to girls' silk stockings. The Gamer Shoe Company offered to have every pair of stockings it sold adorned with a replica of the *Spirit of St. Louis* artwork painted by Thomas Manning, a Butte commercial artist.

The Anaconda paper reported that the novelty of having Lindbergh's plane painted on their stockings "appealed to many of the younger Butte feminine population, judging from the numbers who displayed the decorated stockings last night." The fad was expected to spread to visitors flocking to the Mining City for the

Lindbergh festivities. Gamer expected brisk sales of its Humming Bird and Blue Crane stockings.

It wasn't just a shoe company that latched onto Butte's Lindbergh frenzy. The Home Baking Company, on Olympia Avenue, ran a "Welcome Lindy" advertisement touting its Betsy Ross Bread, "made with Milk from 'All-of-the-Wheat' Montana Flour." Stores in Butte's bustling business district got in the act, too, adorning themselves "in a spirit that reflected the thought of the day—the arrival of Col. Charles Lindbergh."

The display at the Hennessy department store on Main Street stood out. It featured a miniature *Spirit of St. Louis* placed over the main entrance, and "several embryo aviators were given their first taste of flying in the work of keeping the propellors in motion."

A Hennessy store window display included a background that showed Lindbergh's flight across the ocean, symbolized with velvet in the foreground, as well as miniature versions of the *Spirit* plane and a Bible verse.

While Butte store owners bustled to capitalize on the famed visitor's arrival, preparations to accommodate Lindbergh continued at the Butte airport. Officials had set up restricted zones marked by signs and had called in extra police and sheriff's officers, aided by soldiers from Fort Missoula, to keep the field clear and safe. Butte workers had groomed the field into a near-perfect condition, and a large white circle had been painted to guide *Spirit* to earth. Marks indicated the field's boundaries, and a hangar to house the plane stood ready.

Excitement in Butte mounted on the Sunday before Lindbergh's arrival. He did not, however, grab the top headline in one of the local newspapers. That belonged to a story about a "crazed father" who shot and killed seven family members in Youngstown, Ohio. Not far below a stack of streamers about other top news of the day was an all-capital-letters headline that read: "All Is In Readiness For Greatest Celebration Butte Has Ever Known, The Welcome To Lindbergh." Butte's streets, "gay with color and banners," evidenced the Mining City's enthusiasm for the twenty-five-year-old who had captured the heart of the nation and much of the world.

A record attendance at the welcoming banquet seemed assured, and one segment of the populace was deemed especially fixated on Lindbergh.

"The Butte public, particularly the feminine portion, is said to be desirous of seeing him at close range and hearing the message of this remarkable citizen who staked his life in the greatest adventure of all time and calmly waved aside wealth equal to a king's ransom while clinging to his idea of service."

On September 5, 1927, the *Anaconda Standard*, the Marcus Daly-owned newspaper in the nearby town where the Anaconda Company smelter was located, gave Lindbergh's pending arrival that day almost end-of-the-world play in its pages.

" 'Welcome, Slim, the Place is Yours!' Butte's Greeting to 'Lone Eagle' " was the banner atop the front page. Below the flag: "ALL MONTANA TO JOIN LINDBERGH RECEPTION TODAY." Leading into the article were five more headlines, starting with: "Mining City Is Crowded With Visitors Here to Honor Atlantic Conqueror" and "THOUSANDS TO WELCOME HERO AT CLARK PARK." The last three headlines said arrangements were ready for

"Butte's greatest reception"; Lindbergh would parade through the city, and a great day would close with a banquet where hundreds of people would "break bread" with an illustrious guest of the city, then a metropolis of about 100,000 people (including surrounding mining communities) that was the most populous place between the Twin Cities and Seattle.

Lindbergh was greeted in Butte by the man who was the pilot for his 1922 barnstorming run into Montana, J.H. Lynch, who had moved from Billings to Butte after the Billings performance. Lynch was joined by Matt Alexander, one of the Butte airport's owners.

The Standard said Lynch and Alexander would tell Lindbergh that Butte was his for the day. The city had been decorated and was ready to give Lindbergh the "greatest volume" anyone had ever received in Butte. Mine whistles were to let loose "a thundering roar," splitting the air into "a thousand fragments."

Now that Butte's big day had come, it probably calmed the nerves of the head of the city's welcoming committee, who worried that his city would face the same problem that Fargo did when Lindbergh had visited the North Dakota city.

Butte state senator H. A. Gallway, relying on what Jack Lynch said to a local newspaper, cautioned Butte residents to not delay deciding whether they would attend the banquet.

"Up to the time of Lindbergh's arrival, only 150 banquet tickets had been sold" in Fargo, Lynch said. "It really looked as if the banquet were going to be a frost, but within thirty minutes after Lindbergh landed on the field, there was a lively rush for tickets and at night, when the banquet ceremonies opened, there were 1,200 banqueters present."

Gallway reported a rush on tickets for the Butte event during the previous two days. He asked the public to understand the limits to the banquet ball's capacity. It seated 1,500, and it would do Butte proud to have every seat filled. He said it would be unfair for his committee to arrange for a crowd of 1,500 and have only 1,000 show up. The quandary, however, was that event organizers, gauging the likely attendance by ticket sales earlier in the week, might prepare food and seats for 1,000 and have 1,500 show up at the last moment.

"The experience of Fargo should be a lesson to all of us," he said. "The public would render the committee splendid assistance by making Saturday evening the deadline for ticket sales."

The committee could accommodate demand for a modest hundred extra tickets on banquet day, but if the public held off until the final hours before the banquet, then rushed ticket sellers, that would be "annoying," Gallway said.

Boise was Lindbergh's last stop before he pointed *Spirit* north to Butte. An estimated 40,000 people from throughout Idaho saw his visit to the state capital on a Sunday before he took off at 10:30 a.m. on Monday.

In Boise, Police Chief Andy Robinson said he knew Lindbergh's scheduled departure time, but he hadn't made specific arrangements to control traffic. Informed at 10 a.m. on the departure day that an "immense crowd" had gathered at the airport, the chief instructed all available uniformed officers and other plain-clothed officers to rush to the field. They managed to keep "perfect order" among the throng.

"Col. Charles A. Lindbergh, the thunderbird of the Atlantic took Butte by storm yesterday." That started coverage of one of the biggest events to ever occur at "The Greatest Hill on Earth."

Flying north to Montana, Lindbergh "dropped out of a clear sky in his glittering silver plane, the '*Spirit of St. Louis*,' the 'we' of his exploits, on the Butte landing field, only to be immediately taken into the hearts and minds of a populace which turned out en masse to greet the slender, youthful figure whose matchless exploits astonished the people of three continents," as a newspaper account put it.

Thousands greeted Lindbergh at what served as Butte's airport then (now Bert Mooney Airport). A crowd expected to reach 10,000 or more packed Clark Park to hear him speak. And comparable throngs lined the streets to see the parade that took Lindbergh to where he stayed, the Finley Hotel. Hundreds of people dined with him at the Parkway Theater ballroom, while equal numbers packed the street in front of the theater, straining for a sight of Lindbergh and his "whimsical" smile.

When Lindbergh landed in Butte at 1:58 p.m. on September 6, 1927, about 15,000 people were on hand at the city airport, and about 50,000 people saw him during his stay in the booming Montana city.

Committees had been working "feverishly" to make sure Lindbergh received a proper welcome. When the *Spirit of St. Louis* touched down in Butte, it would roll to a stop on an airfield "declared by traveling fliers to be one of the finest in the United States."

Butte spectators were told they would see a "huge" Ryan monoplane. Hyperbole aside, Lindbergh's plane, tiny by twenty-first-century standards, was at best only average size and probably on the small side even in 1927. In case vandals and souvenir seekers showed up, Butte officials had hired guards and erected fences to keep the plane safe.

"That the throng will be representative of the whole state was proved last night, when a number of hotels refused to accept further reservations," their clerks voicing a repetitive refrain: "Filled up; sorry."

Lindbergh, described as being "brown as a bear" by a parade spectator, sat in a big chair for a newspaper interview soon after he landed. He wore a dark, grey suit and a white shirt and had on black shoes that carried dust from the Butte airport.

Lindbergh tried to boost local prospects for a stake in the embryonic commercial airline industry. He said a northern air route was sure to come and Butte should build a modern, fully equipped airport. That topic came up when the reporter learned that Lindbergh, despite his youth (twenty-five at the time), knew how to steer press people to subjects of his interest.

"When one starts an airway through the northern way, it's up to Butte to put up the backing to land on that air map. Butte is quite a logical spot on the route. If Butte doesn't get on it, some other city will," he said. Butte first needed an up-to-date airport, with all equipment airlines would need because "there is no use talking; air travel is a matter that will find development in the next few years in great strides. Therefore, everyone in Butte should get behind commercial aviation," he said.

Discussing local flying conditions, Lindbergh said, "Over the ranges at certain heights it is quite bumpy," but "the super-charged motor ... will be the salvation of the altitude problem." Advances in airplane motor design would allow planes to fly higher and provide smoother travel than on the ground.

One thing more was needed to foster the air industry: Uniform state regulations in accord with the federal system. Otherwise, a patchwork of conflicting state laws "will hamper the development of the science," he said.

Lindbergh preempted an obvious question from his interviewer. No, he didn't plan to immediately make another long-distance flight. The reporter next asked Lindbergh to help him, the reporter, probe some aspect of the Atlantic flight that other newspapers might have overlooked.

"That was four months ago; it's old now, but I don't mind giving you something that's new if I have it," Lindbergh said, showing what was called his famous smile. "About everything has been covered about that flight, I guess, and in fact there were a lot of things I read about it that I didn't know myself."

Lindbergh wore his pilot clothes at the airport and at the park, but he had changed into a business suit for the dinner at the theater. Thus, "his youthful figure and his boyish face were accentuated by the appearance of those who surrounded him, grave, middle-aged and elderly men," creating a scene befitting the saying, "A child shall lead them."

When Lindbergh rose to speak at the banquet dinner, his boyish looks astonished attendees. It had been mere weeks since he became "the hero of the most daring exploit known to history" when "single-handed and alone he faced not only the dangers of death, but a greater mystery still, the possibility of life ..." an inference that Montanans at the function, mostly from Butte but undoubtedly a few from elsewhere, thought they were seeing a miracle in the flesh.

Butte, exhibiting "its characteristic hospitality, its enthusiasm and its whole-hearted welcome," pulled out all the stops for the Lone Eagle.

"Nothing was left undone and nothing was done wrong. Children as well as elders had the opportunity to see the world's greatest hero, and Lindbergh, the idol of youth, carried his message straight to the hearts of the youth of Butte. Even the weather, doubtful for weeks, could not have been more perfect," a local newspaper said.

The Butte banquet for Lindbergh took place in the Parkway Theater ballroom where people clung to every word of his description of the flight three months earlier. "The best talent in Butte" had been lined up for entertainment, and a distinctly Butte gift awaited him: a smoking set, hammered by hand from Butte copper.

Pre-banquet ticket sales indicated that a capacity crowd would attend the event following the flier's speech at Clark Park. Lindbergh headquarters in City Hall scheduled extra hours to accommodate last-minute admission seekers. People who wanted to attend, who hadn't yet purchased tickets, and who were reading the *Standard's* September 5 issue were advised to hurry downtown and get passes first thing that morning. If not, they risked having Lindbergh worshippers from other places snap up the tickets.

Nothing other than Lindbergh was the topic of conversation in Butte on that day. Throngs were expected to come to the airport and strain for a first sight of the *Spirit of St. Louis* in the southern sky. Equal or greater numbers of hero worshippers planned to get to Clark Park early to await Lindbergh's arrival there.

"Children will be favored by the seats at Clark Park," the *Standard* said, and reading the mangled syntax of the paper's writer, it's evident that the community believed youngsters thought and talked of no one but Lindbergh.

"Worshipping him as the greatest hero of the hour, the youngsters impatiently await the moment when they can see him in the flesh and talk to him."

It was, the paper said, Butte's moment to prove that the "old spirit of the West," with its attendant hospitality, still existed and that the Mining City could entertain in royal fashion.

Besides the corporate titans and community leaders who rubbed shoulders with Lindbergh during his Butte visit, a well-known "regular guy" also had a memorable encounter with the "Lone Eagle." That was Elmer Johnson, better known as "Lemons" and described as the Northwest's oldest messenger boy.

Johnson had a ten-minute conversation with Lindbergh, and Johnson "did that which he has not done in years. He did that which he will probably never do again during his lifetime—he drank a bottle of milk."

Weary from the boisterous welcome he had received when he flew into Butte, Lindbergh had retired early to his room at the Finley Hotel. He left instructions with hotel clerk Joe Foley to have his breakfast served at 6 the following morning, when he would get ready to take off for Helena and be a featured attraction at the state fair.

Johnson showed up promptly, rapped on Lindbergh's door, and was greeted by the famous visitor.

"Your breakfast, sir."

"Come in," Lindbergh said.

Foley had heard Lindbergh liked milk, so he sent "Lemons" with four pints of milk to his destination. Lindbergh looked over the offering, then drank two bottles before he turned to "Lemons."

"Friend, I can't drink all of this; you had better join me."

The messenger's eyes opened in amazement at the invitation.

"Partner, you're the only man in the world I'd drink this stuff with," said the Butte man.

Lindbergh laughed as "Lemons" drained a bottle of milk and gazed at the room in a dazed manner. Then Lindbergh showed the infectious all-American attitude he became known for. He found a silver dollar in his pocket and handed it to Lemons.

"If you don't like that stuff, here's a dollar. Go out and buy yourself a real drink."

The messenger accepted the coin. He held it, grinned, then looked at Lindbergh.

"Partner, me, spend this dollar? Not me. I'm going to put this in a frame and I'm going to keep this buck and maybe when I die, my friends will raffle it off and get enough dough to plant me."

Done drinking milk, Lindbergh was set for a flyover above the Montana city with a plant that refined Butte copper into the copper rod, wire, and cable that electrified the United States in the 1920s.

THIRTEEN

Great Falls gala

As Great Falls geared up for the anticipated arrival of Charles Lindbergh, people in Montana's Electric City realized there was no chance that "Slim" would stop in their locality as he flew from Butte to Helena to be honored there at the state fair.

Still, they could delight in knowing that Lindbergh would fly overhead, according to a telegram sent by Donald Keyhoe, the United States Department of Commerce aide assigned to Lindbergh for his tour, to Great Falls Mayor H. R. Mitchell. The wire, sent from Boise, where Lindbergh stopped before flying to Butte, said the celebrated flier would buzz Great Falls and drop an autographed message, urging the city to develop commercial aviation.

Mitchell wired back to Keyhoe, saying that "Great Falls would be honored by the visit and plans were made immediately to notify residents ... of the exact time when the monoplane appeared on the horizon."

Fire Chief A. J. Trodick announced that the progress of Lindbergh's flight from Butte would be monitored and reported by telephone to the fire department. Shortly before *Spirit* was due, a man equipped with field glasses would be sent to the tower at the central station.

"As soon as the ship is sighted, the fire department siren will be sounded and thousands of eyes will search the horizon to the southwest for the first glimpse of 'we.' As the plane reaches the edge of the city, the siren will be blown again and a few seconds later the roar of the motor will be heard over the downtown district."

Keyhoe said Guggenheim Foundation regulations forbade Lindbergh from making stops in cities other than those on the official itinerary. If Lindbergh were to make an exception and land in Great Falls, that would open the floodgates to requests from hundreds of other cities. If he agreed to even some of them, completing the nationwide tour on time would be impossible.

A trip to Great Falls entailed about 200 extra miles of flying, but because *Spirit* could cruise at more than 100 mph, that meant flying time would increase by only about two hours. Although it was unlikely Lindbergh would pass over Helena on his way to Great Falls, this side trip was expected to give residents of small towns on the way a chance to see the historic monoplane and its pilot in the sky.

Great Falls got its moment in the Lindbergh sun on September 7, 1927, when "We," as newspapers now called the pilot and plane, appeared out of the west at 1:15 p.m. An instant later, the siren blared at the Great Northern Railway shops on the west side of the copper smelter and the Central fire station joined the welcoming chorus just before *Spirit* crossed the Missouri River. Other big whistles in town joined the din.

Crowds had gathered, and people scanned the western sky, hoping to catch a first glimpse of the plane, but Lindbergh's arrival was delayed by nearly an hour. Reports said Lindbergh and his Commerce Department escort plane became separated while crossing the mountains between Helena and Great Falls. The escort plane was sighted flying near Cascade, where it circled several times, dipped, and turned back to Helena.

The *Spirit of St. Louis* came into view east of the mountains near Great Falls, but it, too, circled several times before it disappeared. Time passed, then the plane appeared against the skyline west of Great Falls. Lindbergh was flying a course along the Sun River, suggesting that after crossing the mountains, he had flown a little too far north before he saw Great Falls.

Lindbergh crossed the southeastern part of the city, circled over east side and north side residential districts, then banked sharply to drop over the downtown business district. Flying above Third Street, he dropped his usual message. Contained in a canvas bag and attached to long orange streamers, it hit Ingeborg Myre, proprietress of the Peacock shop in the Liberty Theater building, on her shoulder, then fell to the ground. Miss Myre gave the bag to the mayor.

Lindbergh continued south, flying over the First National Bank building, where "a half score of men and women" were standing on the roof. They waved at Lindbergh as he sped past, and he responded with a "snappy salute."

Onlookers could see the "famous Lindbergh smile" above the rim of the cockpit, but he was flying so low—fewer than fifty feet above the roof—that he had to devote all his attention to flying.

Lindbergh flew over the junior high school on First Avenue South, where students had been let out to greet him. They caught his attention and he soared over the school after dropping his message.

Then Lindbergh was off to Helena and the state fair. There was no mistaking his plane as it flew away from Great Falls, its silver sheen visible in the sun, its number, N-X-211, painted in huge figures on the left wing, and the plane's name written at the rear of the motor, where it could be easily read from the street.

FOURTEEN

Helena hubbub

Lindbergh's pending arrival in Helena created a buzz equal to his reception in Butte. Helena's advantage was that it, as the site of the Montana State Fair at the time, gave him a stage that spanned the Treasure State. (The state fair moved to Great Falls in the 1930s and has been held there ever since.)

Officials of the September 1927 event got praise from the hometown newspaper for their decision to offer free admission to the fairgrounds on the afternoon of Lindbergh's visit. The flier's visit had been widely advertised, "and for visitors at the fair not to see him would be unthinkable." Helena's newspaper paper predicted a record attendance for the opening day. After all, Paris, London, and New York had greeted Lindbergh with throngs, so why shouldn't Helena and Montana show up in force?

The fair board decided to give children preference for grandstand seats on "Lindbergh Day." Box seats and other seats required to accommodate the reception committee were set aside, then youngsters below the age of twelve got all grandstand reserved seats. This directive followed the suggestion of Lindbergh's advance man, Milburn Kusterer, who said Lindbergh was especially eager to appear before the younger generation.

As part of Helena's hoopla, Jack Lee wrote a song titled "The Eagle of the Sea." It was on sale, and the Lee vaudeville troop sang the tune during the program.

Local boosters saw the state fair, with Lindbergh

as the headliner, as a boon to the capital city. The *Independent-Record* editorialized a hope that Helena residents would attend the fair in big numbers on Monday and Wednesday of fair week. That would signify a spirit of "cooperation (with) the good citizens from other parts of Montana who will come to Helena Tuesday." Fair officials asked out-of-towners to stay as many days as possible. That way, the state fair would not be "penalized for keeping faith with the people of Montana in bringing Colonel Lindbergh to the fair and in respecting the unbroken wishes of their guest, that his visit not be commercialized in any way."

The IR noted that Montana was the only venue on Lindbergh's tour where he stopped at a state fair.

The excitement stirred by Lindbergh's impending trip to Montana had prompted aviation enthusiasts to stage the Treasure State's first air meet. It took place during the state fair in Helena from September 5-9. At least a dozen planes were expected to participate in daily events, which included parachute jumping, stunt flying, and air races.

The program included four races daily, and pilots competed for first- , second-, and third- place prizes. A state senator from northeastern Montana, J. W. Schnitzler of Froid, planned to have two Ryan monoplanes arrive in Helena just before Lindbergh got to Montana. He planned to have them flown to Butte on the morning of Lindbergh's arrival there, then have those planes escort the Lone Eagle to Helena. Schnitzler's planes came from the same Ryan factory in San Diego that manufactured Lindbergh's Spirit of St. Louis.

Other notable early pioneer Montana pilots expected to participate in the meet included A. W. Stephenson, of Dillon; Earl Vance, of Great Falls; Penn Stohr, of Plains; and Robert Johnson, of Missoula. The buzz also reached North Dakota. James Bowen, a Jamestown man, said he was trying to arrange for two planes and a parachute jumper to come to Helena.

Lindbergh mania even extended to the state's version of the Miss Montana contest at the time. Carter County, in the far southeastern corner of the state, was among thirty-nine counties choosing entrants competing for the Queen of Montana title. The Carter County entrant not only would get to travel to Helena and enjoy the fair but also, if chosen queen, might get a brief encounter with the honored guest.

After four days of "social whirl," on September 8, the young women chose as queen Bertha Ainley, described as a "charming brunette" from Chester, the Liberty County seat. She was crowned at the Lindbergh Day dinner at the Shrine Temple by Governor John Erickson. County princesses were honored guests at the event.

"Fair Opens With Seething Mass on Grounds." That was the newspaper headline that greeted Lindbergh on his arrival in the capital city. A crowd estimated at more than 6,500 came to the first day of what was then the twenty-fifth annual Treasure State exposition.

Lindbergh was scheduled to arrive from Butte at the grounds at 2 p.m. on September 6. Helena residents and visitors were instructed to come to the fairgrounds to see the visitor. They were warned not to gather on roads and streets leading to the airfield at the Municipal Golf course or on the field itself. Lindbergh made it a condition of his appearance that the landing field be clear to avoid accidents. If that stipulation wasn't met,

Lindbergh said he wouldn't land but would turn back to Butte. The reason for the precautions, readers were told, was that Lindbergh used a periscope to fly *Spirit of St. Louis*. He sat in the cockpit behind the fuel tanks, which obscured his straight-ahead view. He worked around that by using mirrors attached to the periscope.

When Lindbergh reached the state fairgrounds, the crowd waiting him, more than 25,000 people, surpassed expectations. The throng was a cross-section of Montana.

"Civil war veterans, world war veterans, city folk and country folk from every corner of the Treasure State filled the grandstand and bleachers to overflowing and the space immediately surrounding the building was a milling mass of humanity, each endeavoring to edge closer to the stand where the hero of the day would soon appear," a newspaper account said.

Spectators saw a "silvery plane" approaching from the south, and murmurs of "Lindbergh" rippled through the throng. The plane momentarily disappeared, then was spotted approaching from the east. The crowd roared as Lindbergh guided his monoplane north of the stands. He circled east, then touched down on the golf course, where Governor Erickson and the state's upper echelon greeted him.

Lindbergh had circled over Helena between noon and 1 p.m. before touching down a few minutes after 2 o'clock. Another plane preceded Lindbergh to Helena; on board were managers of his tour and representatives of the state department of commerce's aeronautics bureau.

"It's Slim. It's the colonel," one of the men in that plane said when Lindbergh's craft was spotted. As he approached Helena, it looked for a while that he might land on the "I," for Intermountain College, painted on Mount Ascension, as he skimmed treetops on the slope. When he landed on the golf course airfield, he touched down so lightly that he hardly raised dust. He taxied to a lot enclosed by a barbed wire and parked his plane there, where it was watched over by Montana National Guard troops.

Spectators had to wait a bit to see Lindbergh. Careful as always, he kept the engine running while he made a final check of his plane. People could see only a brown leather helmet inside. Lindbergh pulled down the right-hand window, seeming to listen to for any sign of engine trouble. Motion picture cameras were clicking, the crowd was cheering, and finally Lindbergh stopped the engine. The grass stopped rushing, and he stepped out, smoothing his hair a bit. He was first introduced to Erickson and Montana congressman Scott Leavitt, then to other dignitaries, among them former governor Sam Stewart and Helena Mayor Percy Whitmer. Lindbergh and others got into a large open Packard car and headed to the fairgrounds. Led by the 163rd Regimental Band, what was described as "the largest crowd ever gathered in Montana for any occasion" awaited the toast of the town.

Erickson introduced Lindbergh, whose address touched on his by then familiar theme that America's cities needed to embrace commercial aviation and take concrete steps to become part of what was sure to become a thriving industry.

"Some of our larger cities have their landing ports five miles or more from the center of town and it requires an hour or more to go this distance," he said. That obstacle to efficiency needed to be remedied for commercial aviation to progress, he added.

Lindbergh reminded his listeners of how much progress already had been made in airplane design. Gone were the days of planes made of bamboo and wire, which couldn't take off when the wind was blowing. Now, pilots were flying all-metal planes that could be flown in any weather. This made air travel comparable and competitive with any kind of transportation, he said.

Lindbergh noted that U.S. aviation included two branches of flying: commercial, which encompassed air mail, air express, passenger service, and the like; and "pioneering" aviation, which involved flying tests, distance flights, and other types of "untried" flying.

"Commercial aviation is safe while pioneering aviation is still hazardous. Mail and express services are the forerunners of a network of passenger lines," he said. He called on his audience, and the American public in general, to support commercial aviation and cooperate in efforts to develop it so it could come into its own.

Governor Erickson followed by saying Montana was having a notable day as host of one of the world's heroes.

"Not many weeks ago an unassuming young man who came out of the west, animated by a pioneering spirit, fired by the zeal with which he went about his chosen profession, set upon a mission such as no American before him had performed. It was his ambition to demonstrate to the world that a non-stop flight from New York to Paris was a possibility of today rather than of some far future time.

"He went about his self-imposed task with no blare of trumpets, with no shouting and tumult, and with little of the publicity that in these days seems so vitally essential to the performance of any out-of-the-ordinary feat."

Erickson compared Lindbergh to those Europeans who crossed the Atlantic in the fifteenth and sixteenth centuries in pursuit of riches and new lands.

"As his forebears sailed the unchartered seas in their voyaging, so our intrepid young hero sailed the unchartered ether, his only outlook the sky above and the limitless expanse of water below."

People were waiting and watching for news of Lindbergh's progress, both in Europe and the United States, and some had already written him off as "another sacrifice to the insatiable God aviation," Erickson said.

Then came electrifying news: first, that Lindbergh had been spotted flying over the coast of Ireland, then that he had landed at Le Borquet Field in Paris.

"He had made his dream come true! He had hopped off with only the laurels of a capable air mail pilot and landed in France to find himself a world hero! He gave greater meaning to the words of the song 'Goodbye Broadway. Hello France.' And by the same token he had, with only his own dauntless spirit and the *Spirit of St. Louis*, written a brilliant page in the history of world progress."

Erickson continued lavishing praise on Lindbergh, pouring out a torrent of words comparable to the flow of the Missouri River after spring melt as it flowed past Helena.

Lindbergh's success had fired the imagination of people everywhere who read about the flight, giving him a level of acclaim that few others had achieved then, the governor said.

Erickson may have spoken more truth than he realized when he continued, saying, "Another state may claim our young hero because of his birthplace, but he belongs to all Americans, because he is the reincarnation of all that America stands for. We have adopted him because of the pride we have in him and that marvelous thing which he modestly did."

Not only had Montana adopted Lindbergh in 1927, but Billings had also taken him under its figurative wings in 1922. In the unknown future, of course, was 1972, when he returned to the state capital, addressed delegates to the state constitutional convention, and urged them to write environmental protections into the forward-thinking document.

Lindbergh had "come home to us," Erickson said, "the same unbridled youth who so short a time ago set out to do—and did—the impossible thing ..."

Lindbergh then spoke, his words greeted with loud applause, then left the speaker's stand, got into a waiting car with his hosts, and was driven to his hotel. He rested there until it was time for the evening banquet.

Meanwhile, fair festivities continued, although some events planned for the program had to be cut due to time limitations. Spectators saw fireworks, three horse races, an airplane race, and something called auto push ball. Entertainment included something termed, using 1920s sensibilities, the Indian squaw race. It involved three ponies, and the winner was the first entrant to cover the half-mile course.

Fair organizers got a break from September weather. A strong wind created a dust storm that completely blurred the field in front of the grandstands, but the storm ended by the time Lindbergh appeared.

Fair officials estimated the crowd that day exceeded 35,000, and they counted almost 3,900 cars parked inside and outside the grounds. Seats in the grandstand were filled by noon, and by one-thirty, the space around the stands and track was packed.

That evening's banquet at the Algeria Shrine Temple attracted 1,200 people. Repeating what he had said earlier upon landing in Helena, and in Butte and every other city on the tour, Lindbergh stressed the need to keep commercial aviation separate from experimental aviation.

"There is no more risk in commercial aviation than in any other means of transportation," he said. "You think there is because all you see from day to day consists of reports about experimental trips."

That impression given by newspaper coverage of experimental trips had nothing to do with the actual state of flying, he said. The purpose of his tour was to convince American cities and businessmen of the need to "(meet) the aviation enthusiasts halfway."

Lindbergh said aviation couldn't succeed without "practical interest" by U.S. cities. "Looking around the country, we know what the necessities are, and you would be surprised to know that the landing grounds are so far removed from some cities that it requires almost as much time to get from the landing field as it does to make the flight from one city to another."

Anticipating skeptics, Lindbergh said he and other pilots often flew at speeds of more than 100 mph. This was their work, and it took planning, "but their aims are defeated—they land fifteen or twenty miles out and the mail or express has to travel by various ways to the city, taking as long to make the delivery from the landing field to the actual delivery point as it would to fly from one city to another."

The banquet was well-organized and "business-like," in the words of the newspaper. A military band was there, and the organizing committee seated Lindbergh in front of vases of sweet peas. Lindbergh, a stickler for punctuality, arrived on time and left on time. He was flanked by the county princesses of Montana but didn't engage in small talk with them.

Banquet attendees dined on a menu of crab cocktail, chilled radishes, olives, and gherkins as appetizers; a main course of cold roast chicken, celery dressing, currant jelly, chipped potatoes, and stuffed tomatoes en surprise; and, for dessert, chocolate eclairs and French apple roll. Coffee, mints, cigars, and cigarettes rounded out the feast.

The organizing committee reached out to one special person, sending a banquet menu to Lindbergh's mother, Evangeline Land Lindbergh, in Detroit. In her thank-you reply, she said she appreciated "a courtesy like this as much as any that can be shown and I thank you sincerely for a souvenir which I shall always be glad to keep."

Lindbergh said he enjoyed the dinner and liked flying over the mountains around Helena. He left the banquet with minimal clatter, departing "just like he arrived, out of a bunch of fleecy clouds—he flew away again and disappeared among the vapors which attend him when he flies across oceans and out of which he has thus far leaped victorious," according to the report given in overblown verbiage.

The Helena banquet over, Lindbergh prepared to fly again. He was scheduled to return to Butte, some ninety air miles away, but he decided to make a side trip. His destination: Billings.

FIFTEEN

Back to Billings

Lindbergh announced the change in his itinerary toward the end of the banquet. As a newspaper commentary noted, "The aviator is said to have a warm spot in his heart for Billings where he became acquainted in the days when he was giving the exhibition flights throughout the northwest."

It had been five years since those summer months in 1922 when Lindbergh and Bob Westover teamed up to give Billings aerial thrills. Now, Lindbergh was a seasoned air mail pilot, an officer in the Army Air service, and the heralded trans-Atlantic flier, yet he still made time to appear in the sky over Billings.

He was scheduled to take off between 9 and 10 a.m., a bit after a U.S. Department of Commerce plane, piloted by Phillip Love, with Keyhoe as his passenger, was expected to leave.

Lindbergh went to bed promptly after he left the banquet at the Shrine Temple. He and his party stayed in a suite on the fourth floor of the Placer Hotel. Their rooms also were once occupied by President Warren Harding, who had died in office. Harding and his wife passed through Helena on June 29, 1923, on their way to Alaska.

Meanwhile, in Billings, the city that would come to call Lindbergh one of its sons, hopes ran high for a triumphant landing by the "Lone Eagle" on this trip through Montana. *Gazette* readers woke up on the morning of September 7, 1927, to an article headlined "Lindy Will Fly Over Billings at Noon Today." Beneath was a sub headline: "May Stop in City; Making Detour to Visit Old Scenes."

In still-smaller headline type, the paper said Keyhoe had indicated that no landing was planned in Billings. Other information from Helena, however, implied that Lindbergh would land in Billings.

"Reports received by the Billings Gazette Tuesday night indicated that Lindbergh may have a surprise in prospect for friends in the city," the paper noted. It got a long-distance telephone call from Helena, saying that Lindbergh was thinking about putting his wheels down in Billings, but that the flier was trying to keep his intentions secret.

"Although acclaimed by the world as a hero without peers, Lindbergh has not forgotten his friends of the days when his every possession was stuffed in the pockets of his greasy coveralls." While at the banquet in Helena, Lindbergh told people that he held "a warm spot in his heart for Billings," and because of that, he would fly 400 miles out of his way (round trip) to again see the place that had been his temporary home five years earlier.

Precedent existed for Lindbergh to deviate from his itinerary. He had decided overnight to visit Pierre, South Dakota, which was not a planned stop in that state. Flying from Butte to Helena, he had swung off course over Glacier National Park and flew over Great Falls, a fortunate detour because he saw the place that became his Montana mountain hideaway, Elbow Lake in the Swan River Valley, on the way.

In the most-publicized example of Lindbergh's independence from the constraints of others, he arrived in New York on a ship after his May landing in Paris. His airplane had been shipped to Washington,

D.C. Nonplussed, Lindbergh, wearing dinner clothes, returned to Washington to retrieve his plane and "later led newspapermen on a merry chase through New York."

Thus, it seemed possible that the *Spirit of St. Louis* would plant its wheels on the Billings soil around noon on Wednesday, September 7. After all, Lindbergh was "his own master" and had time on his hands before he was scheduled to return to Butte and prepare for a "much-needed vacation fishing in Montana."

Bob Westover tried to parlay his relationship with Lindbergh into a Billings bonanza. He wired Lindbergh on September 6, asking him to stop in Billings, but hadn't received an answer to his telegram by the next day. This was considered a good omen that Lindbergh would stop in the city and visit for a few minutes. If a stop in in Billings was impossible, Lindbergh would have wired Westover and said so, the *Gazette* speculated. The reason that Lindbergh wanted to keep a stop in Billings secret, it was thought, was because he didn't want a big crowd to gather at the Billings airfield. That would have kept prevented him from landing, a factor that he warned officials in Butte and Helena about before he reached Montana.

Westover had tried earlier to persuade Lindbergh to add Billings as a Treasure State landing spot, but to no avail. Westover heard from Lindbergh in mid-August and was told a stop in Billings couldn't be added to his strict tour schedule. The telegram that seemed to dash the city's hopes read: "I regret very much that I will not be able to stop at Billings as New York is the only authority for making changes in stops."

Still, Billings people, likely those who were in Westover's circle, believed that Lindbergh would at least fly over the Hogan air strip three miles west of the Billings city limits—the place where, in 1922, Lindbergh climbed aboard Westover's plane several times for exhibitions of wing walking and parachute jumping.

Speculation ending, the Magic City had to settle for a flyover.

"Flying Colonel Back to 'Jumping Ground' of Five Years Ago; City is Thrilled." That newspaper headline appeared above the next-day report of Lindbergh's reappearance in the sky over Billings.

"The visit of the young air hero ... was characteristic of his independent, whimsical way. Precluded from making a stop here, he came hundreds of miles out of his course to drop a message to friends here and thrilled a large crowd at the landing field on the rimrock with the hope that he might after all decide to land."Maybe a touch-and-go there? Nope.

Flying from Helena back to Butte, Lindbergh decided not to take a direct path of ninety or so miles between the two cities. Instead, he pointed the *Spirit of St. Louis* toward Yellowstone National Park. After sightseeing there from the air, he turned north and followed the Yellowstone River to Livingston. Then, he continued down the Yellowstone valley toward Billings. First, someone in Big Timber, eighty miles west of Billings, phoned the *Gazette* about sighting the plane. Lindbergh kept flying high and was spotted by people in Reedpoint and then, just before noon, in Columbus, forty-five miles away.

The first clue that Lindbergh was near Billings came when a plane was spotted over Hesper, then a farming community west of the city. That was N 57,

Love's plane. This prompted workers in Billings to blow factory whistles throughout the city. Love flew over the Cove district, waiting for Lindbergh to arrive.

Lindbergh and Love flew in parallel formation for several miles, then "Slim" peeled off and flew toward the Hogan airfield, where farmer and property owner Ben Hogan had allowed planes to land, among them ones flown by Lynch and Bob Westover in 1922, with Lindbergh on board as a wing walker and parachute jumper.

Spectators on the Rimrocks thought Lindbergh might land there, but after hovering overhead, he rejoined the companion planes. The planes flew toward the heart of Billings, with Lindbergh in the lead.

Love flew south, but Lindbergh dropped low above Billings' downtown buildings. He circled stores and offices four or five times, giving watchers on the streets an excellent view of his plane. When he flew over the Stapleton Building (which still stands on North Broadway), he dropped a message to Billing residents.

Typed except for the heading and signature, which were written in ink, the message was written on a large poster, rolled up and enclosed in a canvas carton and tied with a yellow ribbon. The message bore a photograph of the *Spirit of St. Louis* and said:

"Aboard *Spirit of St. Louis*, on tour. Greetings.

"Because of the limited time and the extensive itinerary of the tour of the United States now in progress to encourage proper interest in aeronautics, it is impossible for the *Spirit of St. Louis* to land in your city.

"This message from the air, however, is sent you to express our sincere appreciation of your interest in the tour and in the promotion and expansion of commercial aeronautics in the United States.

"We feel that we will be amply repaid for all our efforts if each and every citizen in the United States cherishes an interest in flying and gives his earnest support to the air mail service and the establishments of airports and similar facilities. The concerted efforts of the citizens of the United States in this direction will result in America's taking its rightful place within a very short time as the world's leader in commercial flying.

"CHARLES A. LINDBERGH"

The message landed on First Avenue North, between North Broadway and North 29th Street, near the Todd Shoe Company store. It fell near the car of L. C. Riddle of nearby Park City, who took the message to City Hall, then at the corner of First Avenue North and Broadway. Summoned to City Hall, Mayor Art Trenerry received the message and thanked Lindbergh for his interest in Billings.

Done circling the city, Lindbergh and Love flew south to the Yellowstone River. It appeared that Lindbergh was looking for the spot where he launched his leaky boat in October 1922 to start his aborted voyage down the Yellowstone and Missouri rivers to St. Louis.

Lindbergh hovered a bit over the hills south of the river next to wheat fields on a bench, then headed for the rimrocks. Love had already flown over the rudimentary field there and hopes rose that Lindbergh would land.

A long line of cars awaited Lindbergh at the airstrip. Shoemaker, by now manager of the Billings Commercial Club, and County Surveyor C. E. Durland had directed motorists to park so they wouldn't interfere with a possible landing.

A cheer rose from the crowd as Lindbergh approached the field. He flew the length of the field, then raised the plane and circled back. Spectators saw the silver-colored sides of Lindbergh's aircraft gleaming in the sunlight.

"A mechanic's garb of brown, a tall form and a face in shadows could be made out in the plane by those fortunately located. At each low swing, the crowd cheered and invited the master of the air to land."

Lindbergh, however, rejoined Love, and the two pilots made another pass over Billings before turning to the southwest and following the Yellowstone River. Billings bystanders last saw an occasional flash of light as Lindbergh and Keyhoe vanished, headed back to Butte.

Lindbergh's flight along the Yellowstone Valley caught the eye of a Big Timber rancher who wanted to honor the flier after seeing the *Spirit of St. Louis* cruise over his house. Henry Stole said Lindbergh, on the way from Helena to Billings, topped the ridge of the Crazy Mountains, dropped low and crossed a coulee at the Stole ranch, then flew over Tin Can Hill bound for Billings. To honor Lindbergh's flight over his ranch, Stole said he was going to build a landing field on his property.

SIXTEEN

Escape into the Montana mountains

Nearing the halfway point of his cross-country promotional tour, Lindbergh hadn't gotten a vacation. Finally, in western Montana, he found rest and relaxation courtesy of some of the Treasure State's leading businessmen and industrialists.

Lindbergh got away from the bustle that had become his life for five days, September 8-12, 1927, at was then called Elbow Lake. "Famous Aviator Enjoys Rest In Virgin Country. Mountains Bordering Camp Declared Far Superior in Scenic Charms to Anything Swiss Alps Have to Offer," read the *Anaconda Standard* headline that heralded Lindbergh's backcountry trip.

Before he relaxed in the shadow of the Mission Mountains, however, Lindbergh flew the *Spirit of St. Louis* on a scouting trip of Elbow Lake and its surroundings. He heard about the lake when he arrived in Butte on September 6, 1927, from prominent local people who told him about the mountain gem. Lindbergh noted the lake on his flying map, and when he flew to Helena for the festivities there, he traveled by way of the new scenic spot nestled in the Swan Valley. Its stunning beauty and wildlife proved to have an irresistible pull on the twenty-five-year-old flier.

"Arriving over the spot, he swooped low and noted with satisfaction the canoes, motorboats and fishing rafts reposing on the bosom of the lake, the substantial camp buildings, the tents that were being erected and the piles of luggage, reposing under tarpaulins, awaiting completion of the storehouse," *Standard* readers learned

Lindbergh put his camera to good use. He photographed "huge black bears and deer, in the natural pastures surrounding the spot." He captured a photo of a massive white cliff "so high, so remote that it suggested a floating cloud" instead of a stone block poking above the forest.

Atop the cliff, on a perch that extended several feet, with a thousand-foot drop below, stood a "gray old goat." This "patriarch of all the mountain goats in the Western Hemisphere" that had probably never seen an airplane was the start of an anthropic description:

"The animal was looking as astonished as a mountain goat possibly could look, his huge horns resting on his back, his nose pointed at an angle of 45 degrees, his nostrils dilated and his whiskers waving in the wind as he gazed out at the strange man-bird who took his picture as the plane whizzed past the cliff."

After leaving Elbow Lake, Lindbergh continued to look over Montana's mountain majesty. He flew to the Canadian line, likely crossing Glacier National Park, then turned south to fly over Kalispell and Flathead Lake, then went east across the Continental Divide to soar over Great Falls. He arrived back in Helena a little after 2 in the afternoon, having seen a good portion of western Montana in a little more than six hours.

Lindbergh made a ground visit to Elbow Lake two days later, creating a memory of Montana he cherished. His vacation began at 7:30 in the morning on September 8, 1927, the day after he returned to Butte after flying over Billings, and it lasted until he got back to Butte on September 11 and took off for Spokane. Lindbergh's whereabouts in the Swan River Valley hideaway were kept secret from the public as a way of giving him recreation and rest away from the hectic life he had known since returning from Europe in May.

John D. Ryan, chairman of the board of the The Anaconda Company, arranged the outing with help from J. R. Hobbins, Anaconda's vice president. Several Treasure State power brokers went with Lindbergh into the forested camp, including representatives of Montana Power Co., Metals Bank and Trust Co., and a variety of others, such as horse wranglers, a cook , a doctor, and a New York City individual. Lynch came along, as did Charles Staples, well-known in Butte as a boxing "matchmaker" for American Legion matches, a hunting and fishing guide, and, in his younger years, a football and boxing star.

It wasn't easy getting to Elbow Lake. The party drove, walked, and packed there, going through Anaconda, Phillipsburg, Drummond, Woodworth, and Seeley Lake. No car could make the final stretch into Elbow Lake, so a pack train of twenty-five horses hauled in the party and supplies.

It took about six and a half hours of travel to go from Butte to the lake. The party stopped in Seeley Lake, south of Elbow Lake, for lunch at the summer home of C. H. McLeod, president of Missoula Mercantile Co.

Seeing Elbow Lake from the air was one thing. Experiencing it at ground level took Lindbergh's experience to new heights, and he raved about that.

"The scenery of the west is second to none in the world, and that in the vicinity of Elbow Lake is the finest I have ever seen," he said.

While at the camp, Lindbergh fished, canoed, went horseback riding and took part in a nighttime bear hunt, which occasioned one of the practical jokes that Lindbergh was known for. A member of the party heard strange noises in the brush and thought a bear was on his trail. There was none, but he raced to the safety of the camp.

The person's footrace gained impetus when Lindbergh fired four shots from his rife, then shouted, "The gun's jammed! Run for your life!"

Lindbergh and others caught lots of trout. He spent time target shooting with a rifle and pistol, displaying the marksmanship he acquired, and he took long walks in the woods.

Staples described planning for Lindbergh's getaway in the Elbow Lake area that began almost two weeks before he got to Montana. Staples' diary entry for Saturday, April 27, 1927, says that he returned to Butte that day from a trip he and Baba Urlhelm made to Glacier Lake. They hiked 6.3 miles each way, found excellent fishing in the lake at the foot of Mount McDonald in the Mission Range and saw three bears and a deer. Back in Butte, Staples reported on what he and Urlhelm saw to the Anaconda Co.'s Hobbins.

The next day, Hobbins, his boss Ryan, and Staples left Butte to look over Elbow and Glacier lakes. Driving a Lincoln, Mikey Sullivan was the chauffeur for the trip. After lunch on the Blackfoot River and dinner at Holland Lake, they reached their destination and saw three deer.

On Monday, August 29, the party got on horses and rode from Elbow Lake to the top of a ridge about two and a half miles to the west. There, they could see into Glacier Lake.

"Mr. Ryan and Hobbs satisfied with camp site," Staples wrote, and the men traveled to Missoula, where they stayed at the Florence Hotel. Sullivan drove Staples back to Butte the next day (August 30), and he began packing clothes for a trip back to Elbow Lake to set up camp.

Further preparations ensued. Staples worked with a man named Foster (no first name given) to get supplies in Bonner and Missoula, including lumber from the A.C.M. Lumber Camp. They arranged to have the materials trucked to Elbow Lake, where Staples and Foster set up a temporary tent.

Two men joined Staples and Foster on Friday, September 3, 1927, to make a work party. They tackled improvement of the road to the lake that connected with the highway through the Swan Valley, hauling in four loads of gravel, some of it used to fill a mud hole. The group decided to corduroy that section of the road, a 330-foot stretch, by laying down logs perpendicular to the direction of the road.

Staples and his companions stayed busy for the next five days, setting up the camp where Lindbergh and the bigwigs with him would play in the Montana outdoors. They arrived on September 8, but something notable occurred before that. Staples and Foster hiked to Glacier Lake on September 6, got caught in a "big rain," put out their fishing lines and landed forty-five "big" trout that were supposed to be eaten at the camp. After lunch, they went sightseeing, and in their absence, a bear stole and ate the fish.

On September 9, Lindbergh took a hike after lunch. Staples wrote that he "took (a) gun and followed. (I) found him sitting under a large fir tree. He sat there about one and a half hours. I did not disturb him but kept in same territory."

The next day, Staples reported "cool, terrific

thundershowers after lunch." He and Lindbergh each found cover from the rain under canvases, and they fished together for an afternoon.

Topping the day, Staples got Lindbergh's signature. The diary doesn't say what Lindbergh autographed.

Looking back at his backwoods getaway, Lindbergh said the entire trip was "extremely enjoyable."

His every wish and need seemingly catered to during the outing, Lindbergh would have seemed the epitome of an ungrateful outsider had he voiced a single uncomplimentary remark. As the Augusta News put it, "If Lindbergh had not enjoyed himself, it would not have been the fault of his hosts and fellow guests, nor of the game, the scenery and the climate of Elbow Lake." Every provision was made for Lindbergh's comfort and enjoyment. He returned to Butte as an "enthusiastic admirer of Montana scenery," as did Keyhoe.

Seven decades after Lindbergh's visit to Butte and Helena, Staples' daughter, Mary Katherine Staples Lynch, talked about her father's interaction with the flier in a 1999 interview.

She said her father "thought (Lindbergh) was a very quiet man." In a picture taken then, "he's got an overcoat over his arm, and he's still got his tie on. He's out there with all these rough-looking men. They're all presidents of companies, this, that and the other thing," she said.

"Here's poor old lonesome Charles Lindbergh looking at them all, very quiet."

Mary Lynch said her father told her Lindbergh did not like the publicity he was getting, "the hullabaloo" that followed him everywhere.

She thought Lindbergh's trip to Montana was arranged for promotional reasons, "by people who wanted Lindbergh to get more financial backing, to make more trips. The more promotion and publicity we get for Lindbergh, the more back woodsy we make him feel and look," the more people would want to come to Montana as the state's tourism industry started to take off.

SEVENTEEN

"A thing of beauty"

Then it was time for Lindbergh to leave Montana. His next stop: Spokane. However, a Montana city on the way to eastern Washington—Missoula—got a look at him as he headed west. Lindbergh took off from Butte at 11:10 a. m. on September 12, 1927, but he didn't rush out of town. While the Commerce Department plane warmed up, Lindbergh did a few farewell swoops over Butte.

Missoula got into the bidding for a Lindbergh appearance when Mayor R. W. Kemp wired Keyhoe on September 10, 1927. The mayor's question: Could Lindbergh fly over Missoula and, furthermore, if weather delayed his flight west for a couple days, could he swoop over the county fairgrounds on the opening day of the Western Montana fair? the mayor asked.

If Lindbergh did fly over Missoula, the city's school children were promised a recess from class to see the flight. Missoula officials thought this pitch would appeal to Lindbergh, given his desire to interest youngsters in aviation.

Missoula people thought the weather might work in their favor. Inclement weather with fog was forecast, and they believed Lindbergh's managers wouldn't take a chance of having him fly over mountain ranges in such conditions.

A day later, Missoula people became increasingly optimistic that Lindbergh would fly over their city and give residents a good view of the plane and pilot. Local flyers pointed out that Lindbergh's schedule called for six hours of flying time between tour stops, based on an 8 a.m. takeoff from the city he was leaving and a 2 p.m. arrival at his next destination. Thus, Lindbergh would have time for exploring, as he did when he flew from Butte to Helena.

With the flying time from Butte to Spokane listed as three and a half hours or less, he would have time to swoop over Missoula. Lindbergh reportedly had heard good things about Missoula's airport and wanted to see it. Maybe he could squeeze in a touch-and-go if not a full stop.

Unable to honor their wish, Lindbergh gave Missoulians a thrill by circling "every part of the city" and the airport. City Hall had declared September 12 "Lindbergh Day," and residents began streaming to the airport early in the morning, hoping he would land. Cars were parked two deep around two sides of the field as onlookers waited.

Murmurs that Lindbergh and the accompanying plane were approaching rippled through the crowd. People kept their eyes focused toward the eastern horizon where the flyers were coming from. People mistakenly thought one plane was Lindbergh's. Instead, they had seen Love's plane flying over Mount Sentinel. When it continued west, half of the crowd thought it was Lindbergh and that he had gone on without circling Missoula. They started to leave.

Fifteen minutes later, though, *Spirit* slipped through Hellgate Canyon and reached Missoula at 12:20 p.m. Lindbergh circled so low that people could easily read the name of the plane and its numbers.

"Over the north side, over the east side, the west side, then the south side, and again around the entire city, the beautiful ship of the air swept. Banking steeply, dipping and twirling, the silver plane was a thing of beauty to the thousands who beheld it," the Missoulian said.

Youngsters squealed with delight, and on front lawns stood women dressed in aprons, dust caps and other work clothing, watching *Spirit* swoop over neighborhoods.

Lindbergh streaked toward the airport and flew less than 150 feet above the north end. His plane roared just above those standing along the fairgrounds fence. Then, banking almost straight up, Lindbergh turned right and made another half circle. As he flew over the crowd, he tossed out a long canvas packet with a streamer of yellow silk attached to it.

Youngsters scurried to grab the souvenir. It contained a message to Missoula, a message expressing regret that Lindbergh couldn't land there. The message was identical to what he had dropped in Great Falls and Billings a few days earlier.

Mrs. E. H. Riedel, 434 McLeod Avenue, picked up the message and turned it over to H. O. Bell and Joe Miller, officers of the Missoula Aeronautical Association, who gave it to Mayor Kemp.

Missoulians saw Lindbergh wave and smile as he flew over the crowd.

Perhaps because of fog, Lindbergh followed a course above the railroad line between Butte and Missoula. Thus, he flew low enough coming out of a canyon on his approach to Missoula that many didn't see the plane. Railroad superintendent J. H. Johnson, though, had men stationed at vantage points to watch for Lindbergh. When word came that he was closing in on Missoula, whistles blew—the signal that the "world hero was here."

Hundreds of school children were part of the waiting throng. From high school down, they had been released from class. Some were late returning to school that afternoon, and others took the rest of the day off.

Lindbergh was due in Spokane at 2 p.m. local time, 3 in Missoula. A telegram sent him by the Missoula air association was waiting in Spokane.

"Welcome back to Missoula anytime," it read. Twelve years later, Lindbergh would take up that invitation.

One Missoula woman experienced disappointment during the Lindbergh flyover because she was unable to give him a lunch basket she had packed, hoping to offer it to him at the airport if he landed and got out of his plane. A newspaper report said the woman, "whose hair was streaked with gray," said she had a son "who was always hungry at that time of day." Because Lindbergh was expected in Missoula over the lunch hour, she went into action.

"When I got the morning paper and saw that he would leave Butte at 11 o'clock, I immediately prepared the lunch and rushed out here with it," she said to friends. Lindbergh kept flying, the lunch offered in vain.

As Lindbergh was leaving the Treasure State, the manager of his tour thanked Montanans for the reception they gave him. Keyhoe said organizing committees in Butte and Helena followed the guidelines established before the national tour began in July.

"In Butte and in Helena the people realized that elaborate programs would tire Colonel Lindbergh unnecessarily and held the sort of programs which would permit the colonel to rest and at the same time accommodate the largest number of people."

Asked about the greatest problem faced during the tour, Keyhoe said it was keeping landing fields clear of people.

"We have come into landing fields to find that a crowd of 300 people were grouped inside the space where Colonel Lindbergh was to taxi his plane."

Situations like that arose when members of a local reception committee were told by the committee chairman that they could meet Lindbergh right after he landed. That set up the expectation that they could stand next to the plane and shake hands with him as soon as he stepped out.

Lindbergh got to Spokane on time—actually, a minute early at 1:59 p.m. Several thousand spectators greeted him, including hundreds of schoolchildren and Washington Governor Roland H. Hartley, a Minnesotan who told the flier that he had known his father. Lindbergh stayed overnight in Spokane, then left for Seattle to continue his counterclockwise swing through the United States.

Butte and Helena represented roughly the halfway point on Lindbergh's goodwill tour. They were the forty-second and forty-third cities where he landed in *Spirit*. The tour lasted three months, from July 20 until October 23, 1927, and covered 22,350 miles. Lindbergh visited eighty-two cities in all forty-eight states. He gave 147 speeches, rode 1,290 miles in parades and was seen by more than thirty million Americans—one-fourth-of the country's population. He flew over dozens of cities, including three in Montana. Lindbergh made the tour on behalf of the Daniel Guggenheim Fund for the Promotion of Aeronautics.

The tour also boosted sales of Lindbergh's first book, *We*, an autobiography rushed into print by G. P.

Putnam's Sons. It sold more than 650,000 copies in its first year on the bookshelves, earning Lindbergh more than $250,000.

"Slim" began his tour on July 20, 1927, with a flight from Mitchell Field, the Long Island airstrip where he had taken off for Paris two months earlier, to Brainerd Field in Hartford, Conn. About 500 people saw him take off, and a crowd of more than 30,000 awaited him in Hartford.

Lindbergh finished his trek in late October 1927 when he landed at the Philadelphia City Airport. By then, he had logged 200 hours in the air, had dropped 192 messages to cities he flew over without landing (including three in Montana) and had been feted at 69 dinners and had shaken the hands of governors at twenty-three state capitals.

EIGHTEEN

1928

A year after Lindbergh flew over Billings as part of his triumphant 1927 cross-country tour, the Magic City pulled out the stops and capitalized on his name for an event that would shape its transportation future. "Lindbergh fever" manifested itself in the spring of 1928 when Billings prepared to break ground for construction of its airport atop the Rimrocks.

"Stage Set for Big Aerial Circus on Rimrocks Today" read a newspaper headline trumpeting the late-May event. Readers were told that a parade of twenty planes would open a "monster Lindbergh Day celebration." The event was expected to draw thousands of spectators. Many pilots from outside Billings were expected to fly in.

A week earlier, the stage was set when local officials obtained an option on 400 acres atop the rims for an airfield that still serves as the city's airport.

They immediately decided to capitalize on Lindbergh's fame. The Billings Commercial Club's aviation committee invited pilots and aviation company representatives from inside and outside Montana to attend the circus. Telegrams of acceptance rolled in, causing the committee to forecast a "record crowd" at the airfield site when the event began at 12:30 p.m.

Spectators paid an unspecified "nominal" charge to get on the grounds, with the proceeds to be funneled into airfield improvements. People could buy tickets downtown or on the road to the field, today known as North 27th Street. The highway was changed to a one-way road for two hours on May 28 to better handle the traffic.

Billings pilots and local businessman W. H. MacDonald headed the afternoon program. It included stunt flying, wing walking, and a parachute jump.

About 5,000 people watched the celebration, and thirteen planes, flown at various times by eleven pilots, furnished entertainment. A dramatic display that opened the program featured Charley Spear, a city traffic officer, who volunteered to make a parachute jump. He replaced a boy originally slotted for the jump who lost his courage. People "awaiting a spectacle" got their wish "as the figure of a man slumped from the wing of a plane and hurtled toward the earth, a ribbon of white trailing behind," that being Spear, a former Army parachute jumper.

The crowd murmured "here he comes" as the swath of white appeared, then the parachute billowed into a canopy that carried Spear safely to the ground.

"Charley Spear, waving a hat delightedly, dropped rapidly to the ground. He landed on a hummock of earth far across the field from the crowd which was acclaiming him. He landed hard, fell over backwards and the breath was knocked from him," according to the newspaper account.

Spectators rushed across the field despite the efforts of guards to control the crowd. Spear recovered his wind, climbed aboard his motorcycle, and tried to ride away in its sidecar. The crowd swarmed him so much that it was hard for him to escape.

"I didn't want the crowd to be disappointed," he said.

That year, 1928, also saw creation of a lasting link to Charles Lindbergh's time in Montana, the renaming of a lake in the northwest part of the state, about eighty miles south of Glacier National Park. For the first three decades of the state's existence, the map showed Elbow Lake, a sparkling, mountain basin in the Swan River Valley, with the Mission Mountains to the west. The lake, about four and a half miles long and one-fourth to three-fourths of a mile wide, became Lindbergh Lake when the United States Geographic Board met and approved the name change.

Lindbergh's visit to western Montana, which led to the name change, came about largely due to the influence of Ryan, who besides being chairman of the board of directors of the Anaconda Company was a member of the Guggenheim Foundation board. That organization underwrote Lindbergh's "goodwill tour" to boost commercial aviation throughout the United States. Ryan's son, John C. Ryan, was assigned responsibility for entertaining Lindbergh while he was in the state.

Assistant District Forester L. C. Stockdale announced the name change, saying it was prompted by many letters from the public urging geographic board action.

NINETEEN

A question of loyalty

In 1939, just before the U.S. entered World War II, Charles Lindbergh made his first flight into Billings in twelve years and spent his first on-the-ground time in the city in seventeen years. In 1927, he flew over the city without landing, and in 1922, he lived for three months in Billings as a wing walker and parachute jumper.

Lindbergh's July 1939 flight across Montana, with stops in Missoula and Billings, was part of his survey of the country's aviation facilities, which was commissioned by Major General Henry "Hap" Arnold, head of the Army Air Corps, who reported to Secretary of War Harry Woodring.

Lindbergh left Boeing Field in Seattle at 8:25 a.m. local time (an hour earlier than Missoula) and arrived in the western Montana city one hour and fifty minutes later. He averaged 225 miles per hour for the 415-mile trip. When Lindbergh landed, he called Fort Missoula to arrange refueling with high-grade gasoline. It took ninety-seven gallons to fill his plane's three tanks.

Before he landed, Lindbergh scouted the field by circling it twice. He saw grass at one end and also looked over the runways. After he landed, Lindbergh, his trademark grin visible, said he had encountered gopher holes on another western field and wanted to make sure he wouldn't repeat that problem in Missoula.

Lindbergh was in Missoula for about an hour before he took off in his fast, all-metal Army pursuit plane, a Curtiss P-36. Lindbergh touched down at 11:15 a.m.

in what the local paper called a "pretty landing." The only advance notice that he would stop in Missoula came in an Associated Press dispatch a short time before the "thundering motor of his Army plane was heard above the city." The AP bulletin said Lindbergh had left Seattle that morning without disclosing his destination or plans, although Seattle officials reportedly thought he would make a refueling stop in Missoula.

About thirty-five people were at the airport and saw Lindbergh land. They watched as the "Flying Colonel," dressed in a "trim Army uniform," climbed out of the cockpit to be greeted by H. O. Bell, chairman of the Missoula County airport board.

By the time Lindbergh's plane was refueled and he was ready to take off, word of his appearance had gotten out. A crowd of more than 250 people had gathered at the airport, and a steady stream of cars headed in that direction.

"Cameras appeared by the dozen with shutters clicking almost constantly to get a shot of the distinguished visitor," according to a newspaper report.

Those who overheard Lindbergh said his conversation showed a slight British accent, the result of several years that he and his wife, Anne, spent in England with their two young sons, Jon and Land. He declined to discuss anything other than the task of refueling his plane. The colonel would say nothing of where he'd been, where he was going, or of his plans, saying he had "adopted a policy I can't break of making no statements for publication."

Lt. Col. Earl Landreth, the new Fort Missoula commander, came to the field and invited Lindbergh to noon dinner at the post. Lindbergh declined the offer, saying that because his plane was not equipped for night flying, he wanted to travel as far east as possible during the daylight hours.

One of those who greeted Lindbergh was Captain L. E. Wilson, head of the Civilian Conservation Corps in nearby Superior, Montana. Wilson and Lindbergh had gotten to know each other at an Army airport in Jacksonville, Florida. First Lieutenant Joe E. Golden of Fort Missoula was also part of the welcoming delegation.

The *Missoulian* reminded readers of Lindbergh's previous visit to Montana in September 1927, when he flew over Missoula, Billings, and Great Falls, and landed in Helena and Butte for official stops on his U.S. tour after the trans-Atlantic flight. Upon leaving Missoula this time, Lindbergh inspected his parachute before getting into the cockpit. He grinned and waved to the crowd, circled the field once and made a power dive, dropping to within twenty or thirty feet of the ground, according to the paper. Then he flew on to Billings.

When Lindbergh reached Billings, he caught up with someone as influential as anyone in his progression from barnstormer to famed pilot, the former boss and friend whom he had met in 1922, Bob Westover. Their brief meeting at the Billings airport was captured by the *Laurel Outlook*, the newspaper in the town immediately west of Billings.

In fact, two generations of the Westover family became part of Lindbergh's circle in 1922. Westover's son, also named Bob, was a youngster when he got to know Lindbergh during his stay in Billings. By 1939, Bob Westover Jr. was an assistant cashier at a Laurel bank.

The Outlook said the senior Westover had a hunch

Lindbergh was coming to Billings on July 6, 1939, but he had no definite word. Westover went home from his garage in downtown Billings at around noon, then the telephone rang. It was Lindbergh calling to say he was at the Billings municipal airport, atop the Rimrocks, about two miles from the heart of the city. Westover hurried to the airport. There weren't many bystanders yet, although Billings residents, alerted to Lindbergh's arrival by an announcement on KGHL radio, were driving up to the airport to see the famous visitor.

Billings onlookers saw Lindbergh wearing a regular army service uniform with no decorations other than an insignia on his cap. He wore a flying helmet when he got out of the plane.

About 100 people were at the airport when Lindbergh landed. By the time he was ready to leave, "scores of additional persons were on the way to the flying field."

Here's what happened after Westover got to the airport:

"Lindbergh was in the administration building at the airport, talking casually with a small group of pilots when Westover came in. The two friends exchanged greetings, as they shook hands and Westover said, 'I don't know whether to call you Colonel or Slim.' Lindbergh said something to the effect that 'you can forget about the Colonel part.' "

Lindbergh excused himself from the conversation he had been having with the other pilots. "I'll be seeing you," he said to them, turning toward Westover. The brief conversation between the longtime friends consisted mostly of Westover answering Lindbergh's questions about pilots and other people Lindbergh had known in Montana almost two decades earlier.

"What pleased me most," Westover said afterward, "was that he has not changed. Although he is now thirty-seven years old, he looks like twenty-five. He is still slim despite having put on just a little more weight. The position and fame he has achieved has not gone to his head. He is just like he used to be."

Lindbergh and Westover moved into the airport restaurant, sat down, and chatted a few moments, then Lindbergh signaled his need to go.

"Well, I'll have to be moving along," he said. The two walked outside to where Lindbergh's plane was parked. Lindbergh had fueled in Missoula and had enough fuel to fly to Minneapolis, but he took on more gasoline in Billings, an apparent indication of his continuing affection for the city. Westover watched Lindbergh get ready to take off and continue east.

Although "a seeming daredevil," Lindbergh maintained his practice of taking no avoidable chances when flying. He inspected the plane, tested the engine, and checked everything required for safe flying. Then he taxied to the end of the runway, took off into the prevailing west wind, circled, and flew into an eastern blue sky.

By 1939, Billings was a scheduled stop on Northwest Airlines' routes between the Twin Cities and Seattle, and two passenger planes, a Douglas and a Boeing, were on the runway when Lindbergh landed. He waited for them to take off, then sped down the runway and pointed his plane toward his next stop at Bismarck, North Dakota. As he took off from Billings, Lindbergh swung his Curtiss in a semicircle over the airport and dipped the wings three times.

In his *Wartime Journals*, Lindbergh said that after

leaving Billings, he detoured slightly to fly through the edge of a violent storm in Eastern Montana.

"It lay two or three miles to the north of my course, but flying had been so monotonous after I left Billings that I decided to fly over to it. I could see lightning strike the ground, and rain whipped heavily on the windshield as I flew through the edge. I could just see a little town below, almost blotted out by the rain."

Lindbergh landed at Fargo, North Dakota, at 4:44 p.m. Mountain time. He refueled and took off at 6:24 Central time, pointing his plane to Little Falls and continuing a mission announced in April 1939. Lindbergh reached his boyhood hometown by evening of the day he left Seattle. At Little Falls, he circled Lindbergh State Park before flying to nearby Camp Ripley. He was the overnight guest of Major Ray S. Miller, commander of the 109th Air Squadron, Minnesota National Guard, which was stationed there. He left Camp Ripley the next morning for an undisclosed destination.

Lindbergh's first-hand knowledge of Germany's aerial fighting capabilities, likely unique in the United States, made him invaluable to the military. Thus, he was "called to the colors for active duty with the War Department...in connection with the vast expansion of the Army Air Corps..."

Lindbergh and his family—his wife, Anne, and their two young sons, Jon and Land—had just returned to the United States after several years of voluntary "exile" in Europe. They took up residence in England and Great Britain to avoid the massive press attention that had hounded them in the years after the 1932 kidnapping and death of their first-born child, Charles, and the publicity onslaught that surrounded the trial, conviction, and execution of the infant's murderer, Bruno Richard Hauptmann.

Woodring and Arnold had given Lindbergh responsibility for surveying all aviation research facilities available to the army. His work was under the auspices of the National Advisory Committee for Aeronautics (NACA), the predecessor of National Aviation and Space Agency (NASA).

When Lindbergh completed the survey, he was expected to make a confidential report to Arnold, Woodring said. The report "probably would incorporate all pertinent information on European flying strength which (Lindbergh) gathered during his stay and travels around the continent."

Lindbergh already had submitted a secret report to federal officials. It described "the formidable might of Nazi Germany's air fleet (and urged) that the United States speed up its aviation and research and development if it was to keep up with advances made in the war aviation field by the totalitarian powers."

Lindbergh had provided the same information on Adolf Hitler's growing aerial power to the British government. That purportedly led the British and French to capitulate to Hitler's demands at the Munich Conference in the fall of 1938.

Lindbergh also delivered information about the Soviet Union's air force to Washington, based on his inspection of Stalin's capabilities in the Communist country.

The United States was ramping up its military aviation capabilities when Lindbergh was summoned to Washington. Legislation authorizing expansion of the country's first-line military air fleet, then 2,320 planes, by another 584 planes had passed Congress. A few hours before announcing Lindbergh's assignment, the War Department said it would add 400 "qualified" pilots to the Air Corps to keep pace with the expansion program. Exams for new officers were scheduled that year.

Lindbergh's influence on Montana was again felt in the summer and fall of 1941 as the United States moved closer to entering the global conflict. This effect resulted from Lindbergh's unchallenged status as the world's leading expert on aviation, but it manifested itself in a way that was controversial then and remains controversial today.

Charles Lindbergh was the public face of America First, the nationwide group of prominent public figures who opposed Franklin Roosevelt's efforts to aid first the French and British and then Britain alone in its battle against Nazi Germany and Mussolini's Italy after France surrendered. America Firsters, Lindbergh prominently among them, saw measures such as Lend-Lease and the weakening of U.S. neutrality policy as part of FDR's calculated plan to draw the United States into another resource-draining European war.

England's geography as an island just off the coast of France meant "she cannot win the war by aviation alone regardless of how many planes we send her," Lindbergh said.

"Even if America entered the war, it is improbable that the allied armies could invade Europe and overcome the Axis powers."

Lindbergh said England was clinging to the hope that the United States would rescue her with financial and military resource. Otherwise, "I believe that England would have negotiated a peace in Europe many months ago and be better off for doing so."

Nothing drew more fire toward Lindbergh than the speech he gave on September 11, 1941, in Des Moines, Iowa. It rated just Page 7 coverage in Billings' daily newspaper a day later in an article headlined "Lindbergh Charges Roosevelt, Britain and Jews Are Pressing U.S. Toward War."

Speaking to a Des Moines crowd estimated at 7,500, Lindbergh became notorious for his charge that "the three most important groups which have been pressing this country toward war are the British, the Jewish and the Roosevelt administration." He charged them and other "war agitators" with conducting a step-by-step campaign to nudge the United States into war against Germany and Italy.

"They planned: first to prepare the United States for foreign war under the guise of American defense; second, to involve us in the war, step by step, without our realization; third, to create a series of incidents which would force us into the actual conflict.

"Only the creation of sufficient 'incidents' yet remains; and you see the first of these already taking place, according to plan—a plan that was that was never laid before the American people for their approval."

Lindbergh's remarks prompted boos and cheers. A package of America First cards thrown from the balcony struck and knocked down a plant in a vase directly in front of Lindbergh. Meanwhile, Roosevelt, who gave a radio address heard over loudspeakers at the same time as Lindbergh's Des Moines speech, drew cheers from the crowd eleven times.

Lindbergh said England, then valiantly holding off Germany's Luftwaffe in the epic Battle of Britain, was in "desperate" straits. He said England's army was not large enough nor strong enough to invade Germany.

Lindbergh said he understood why Jews sought the overthrow of Adolf Hitler's regime. "The persecution they suffered in Germany would be sufficient to make bitter enemies of any race. No person with a sense of the dignity of mankind can condone the persecution of the Jewish race in Germany."

Instead of pressing for war, however, American Jews "should be opposing it in every possible way, for they will be among the first to feel its consequences," Lindbergh said, adding a somewhat puzzling statement that tolerance "cannot survive war and devastation."

Six days after the Des Moines speech, Montana's senior U.S. senator, crusading progressive Democrat Burton Wheeler, came to Billings to deliver the last in a series of antiwar speeches throughout Montana. Wheeler was famed for, among other things, helping to expose the Teapot Dome scandals during the administration of Republican President Warren Harding in the early 1920s. Wheeler's appearance at the junior high school auditorium was reported in an article headlined "Wheeler Challenges Roosevelt Order To 'Shoot On Sight.'"

Wheeler, originally a strong ally of FDR but now labeled an isolationist and a staunch critic of his foreign policy, told the audience that packed the auditorium that if Roosevelt intended to take the country into the battles raging in Europe and Asia, "then let it be done in the constitutional way and not in the manner of the Hitlers and the Stalins and the Mussolinis."

Wheeler drew a mix of boos and "resounding cheers." The boos grew louder when Wheeler called Lindbergh "a great American" whose freedom of speech was being denied by Roosevelt administration efforts to keep him from speaking in opposition to possible war.

Billings Mayor Charlie T. Trott, who introduced Wheeler at the start of his speech, which was nationally broadcast by radio, said he disagreed with the senator's stance on war preparedness and the principles of the America First committee. Trott said some Billings people felt the school board should have turned down Wheeler's request to speak in the junior high school building. But displaying a commitment to both First Amendment principles and hospitality, Trott noted his differences with "those who think their mayor does not represent the opinions of this community when he consented to perform the simple act of courtesy (in) extending a welcome of the community to a very distinguished guest."

Fallout from Wheeler's Billings speech included a claim that he dodged a barrage of eggs thrown from the audience. Future Billings mayor Willard Fraser, chairman of the local America First chapter (a widower by then, and the son-in-law of poet Robert Frost, whose daughter, Marjorie, Fraser married and who had died when their only child was born), denied the reports, which he said were both published and broadcast on the radio. Fraser said the reports were "grossly exaggerated and on the whole absolutely fictitious and false, as any in the estimated 2,000 persons in the audience can testify."

Fraser, seated with Wheeler and his wife on the auditorium stage during the speech, said he saw just one egg thrown or rolled onto the stage while Wheeler was speaking. A small boy threw the egg, which grazed Wheeler's coattail and landed well behind him. The senator was unaware of the egg "missile" launched his way until the after the program, Fraser said.

Charges that Lindbergh was a pro-Nazi anti-Semite persist to this day. Perhaps the best assessment of the delicate cakewalk that Lindbergh undertook can be found in what is considered his definitive biography, published in 1998 by A. Scott Berg, who was awarded the 1999 Pulitzer Prize for the volume. Here's what Berg wrote:

"In truth, Charles Lindbergh was never associated with any pro-Nazi or anti-Semitic organization, he never attended any Bund meetings; and since more than four months before the outbreak of war in Europe, he had neither consorted nor consulted with anyone known to have any connections with the Third Reich.

"When Truman Smith (a U.S. military attaché Lindbergh had gotten to know during his days in Berlin) invited him to meet a visiting German dignitary, Lindbergh declined, noting: 'I have had no communication with Germany, or with German citizens, since I left Europe in April 1939, and I think it is important for me to be able to say this whenever the question arises. It is a stupid situation, and I do not intend to govern my actions by such considerations indefinitely, but I do not want to give my enemies any unnecessary opportunity to cause confusion in the public mind at this time.' "

Some years after viewing Nazi death camps when the war ended, Lindbergh decried "some irrational quality" of Hitler, which combined with his actions and oratory mesmerized the German nation into blind support. Yet Lindbergh never acknowledged that he, too, had been under Hitler's spell.

It was Anne Morrow Lindbergh who said that "the worst crimes of the Nazis were not known until after Pearl Harbor and some not until the end of the war or even until the Nuremberg trials." She admitted that she and her husband "were both very blind, especially in the beginning, to the worst evils of the Nazi system."

TWENTY

War and peace

Japan's surprise attack on Pearl Harbor on December 7, 1941, changed everything, for almost everybody, including Lindbergh, Wheeler and Fraser. Lindbergh became a solid supporter of the war effort and served as a civilian advisor to the Army Air Force in the Pacific theater. Wheeler supported the declaration of war, saying, "The only thing now to do is to lick the hell out of them (the Japanese)."

Fraser and the Billings America First committee immediately became backers of the anti-fascist battle, too. On Monday, December 8, 1941, Fraser sent a telegram from Washington, D.C., to H. H. Miller, vice-chairman of the Billings group.

"War, which we have tried so to desperately to avoid, is now our nation's lot. Proudly and without reservation we share a common danger to America. Let no man mistake the fact that we of Montana America First are loyally and courageously springing to the support of President Roosevelt and America. This war is our war and we of America First shall not be found wanting," Fraser said.

Lindbergh faced an uphill battle to restore his reputation once World War II began. He had resigned his Air Corps commission in 1941, believing his integrity as a member of the military would be in question because of his antiwar stance. Once the U.S. declared war on the Axis powers, however, he was ready to serve his country and asked for reinstatement into the Army. His request was denied by President Roosevelt, whose administration, in a fit of pique, forced Lindbergh's aviation employers, including Pan American Airways, to cancel his advisory positions.

One man stood by Lindbergh. Henry Ford asked him to come to Detroit as a technical consultant, helping to convert the Willow Run factory from auto production to production of B-24 Liberator bombers.

In January 1944, Lindbergh made plans to leave for the South Pacific as a civilian technical representative. He left the United States in April that year and flew fifty combat missions. On one of them, a Billings man, who was serving in the Army Air Force in the Pacific, saw him flying a fighter plane.

Al Jenkins said he and his fiancé, later his wife, were having a picnic at what was then called the Indian Caves, now Pictograph Cave State Park, southeast of Billings, on a warm December Sunday. The idyllic outing turned serious when the radio in their Pontiac blurted out the news of the Japanese attack on Pearl Harbor.

Jenkins knew he had to do his part to "whip the Japanese," so the next day, Monday, December 8, 1941, he went to a recruiting office to sign up with the Army. He served thirty-five months overseas.

Sent to Australia as an armament specialist, Jenkins worked on P-38, P-39, and P-47 fighter planes. One morning, he and his fellow servicemen woke and "saw (a P-38) doing every stupid maneuver they couldn't do in the air, and we couldn't figure it out."

The P-38 pilot "came and did dive bombs and almost hit the ground and then pull out and peel off. We couldn't figure it out."

Jenkins and the others were seeing Lindbergh in action.

"Lockheed sent him out," Jenkins said, adding a booster on the P-38 ailerons to give them more maneuverability. "The new P-38s that were coming in were already fitted with this new deal, and Lindbergh was showing them how to operate it."

Lindbergh officially wasn't supposed to fly in combat, but he showed Army Air Force pilots skills they would need to battle Japanese Zeros—and he got in some licks against the enemy, too. All under the official Washington radar.

In 1954, Lindbergh won the Pulitzer Prize for *The Spirit of St. Louis*, his book about the trans-Atlantic flight, and that year President Dwight Eisenhower restored Lindbergh's commission and appointed him a brigadier general in the Air Force.

TWENTY-ONE

Casting a shadow in Montana

The Lindbergh name gained further renown in Montana in 1965, and the resulting acknowledgment of Charles Lindbergh's family's positive influence on the state continues to this day. In April of that year, Charles and Anne Lindbergh's two oldest sons became owners of a historic ranch in western Montana.

Jon and Land Lindbergh bought the 23,000-acre Greenough Ranch in the Blackfoot Valley east of Missoula from William Duce, a rancher and Los Angeles attorney. The ranch had been established decades earlier by Thomas L. Greenough, who also built Missoula's Greenough Mansion.

Land Lindbergh, then twenty-seven, planned to make the ranch a home for him, his wife, Susan, and their two children. They intended to raise Angus cattle on the spread. The two younger Lindberghs established the venture with Land as manager of Lindbergh Cattle Co. and Jon, a marine biologist with Union Carbide in Seattle, working part-time on the ranch. Although he had grown up steeped in his father's flying feats, Land said aviation wasn't the career path he desired. In fact, he didn't have a pilot's license in 1965.

The ranch was a short drive from Lindbergh Lake, formerly Elbow Lake and renamed in 1928 in honor of their famed father's flight. Land Lindbergh later said it was a coincidence that he and his brother bought property so close to their father's namesake lake.

Charles Lindbergh, who became increasingly

wary of publicity after the turmoil of the 1930s, made an under-the-radar visit to Montana in the spring of 1971. He was in the company of *New York Times* reporter Alden Whitman, who wrote about a two-week trip by plane that he took with the flier. The trip was intended to show Whitman "some of the environmental breakdowns" Lindbergh had seen from the sky, and it extended from the East Coast to Hawaii.

Continuing his habit when visiting the Treasure State, Lindbergh took the *Times* reporter to the place where Land began ranching in the mid-1960s and close to where he still lived as a retiree in 2022.

Noting that Lindbergh, then sixty-nine, was a nonsmoker and nondrinker who had never contracted anything but minor illnesses, Whitman wrote that Lindbergh was in "superb" physical shape.

"Six feet 2 and 185 pounds, he is trim and muscular. Without huff or puff, he can walk for miles over rough ground—which he often does on his son Land's Montana ranch."

Land recalled a time, a few years earlier, when he and he and his brother, Jon, had a footrace with their father—and the senior Lindbergh outran both of his sons. "And he probably still can," Land said. Lindbergh claimed that he seldom got tired, something that his family gently differed with and used as a friendly joke. He did, however, admit to getting sleepy now and then, prompting him to take catnaps and awake refreshed.

When Whitman and Lindbergh came to the ranch, it was calving time. Charles Lindbergh insisted on taking one of the two-hour watches to check on pregnant cattle—and not just any watch. He insisted on the midnight watch. He dozed off at 10 o'clock and got himself up at 11:30 p.m. for the duty that every beef-raising ranch and farm family in Montana is familiar with.

Whitman wrote that Lindbergh "seemed disappointed that no calves were born on his tour of duty. He was prepared, though, for when Land suggested there could be trouble—a breech presentation, for example—that prompted his father to reply, 'You know this wouldn't be the first time I've helped cows calve,' "an apparent reference to his boyhood years on his father's Minnesota farm.

In 2022, Land Lindbergh, now eighty-five and retired, looked back at the purchase he and his brother made fifty-seven years earlier. "It was not a particularly good investment. This is hard country to raise cows" because of long winters and deep snowfall, he said.

Sometime after 1927, Montana got a memento of Lindbergh's trans-Atlantic flight. It was a replica of the *Spirit of St. Louis* that got to the Treasure State and was stored for years there before being found in 1971 and taken to San Diego.

Lindbergh looked over the model in late 1972 at San Diego's Air and Space Museum. Lindbergh said the reproduction was the best one ever made, according to his flying friend T. Claude Ryan. Ryan had been an executive at Ryan Aircraft Corporation, which built the plane Lindbergh flew across the Atlantic in 1927.

"He picked out these little things. The exact location of the compass was a little off. The spinner on the propeller was one that the airplane had originally been equipped with but had been replaced in New York, so the one that actually flew across the Atlantic was different. He spotted that right away," Ryan said.

Lindbergh had come to San Diego for a meeting

of the Citizens' Advisory Council on Environmental Quality. He insisted that committee members take time to visit the museum. There, Lindbergh spotted the original M1 monoplane on which he had trained before he took off from New York's Roosevelt Field.

"We found it in a barn on a ranch in Montana about a year ago and restored it," said Ryan, then almost seventy-five but still the board chairman of Teledyne Ryan.

"It was what attracted Lindbergh to our company. It's very similar to the *Spirit of St. Louis* but smaller. He liked the Ryan MI and he spent quite a bit of time in San Diego while the Spirit was being built, to get accustomed because it was so similar."

It was also 1972 when Lindbergh played a key role in the drafting of Montana's new state constitution. Ratified by Montana voters that year, the advanced document is considered by legal scholars to be among the best state constitutions in the country—if not the best. It replaced the constitution enacted when Montana became a state in 1889, a document widely viewed as giving untrammeled clout in Montana to the Anaconda Company, Montana Power Company, and other corporations. Those corporations kept the state in a near-colonial status, with little regard for citizen rights, for more than eight decades.

Lindbergh's pivotal appearance occurred in February 1972, at the state constitutional convention. His visit to Helena is credited with helping empower convention delegates to enact language in the constitution that enshrined Montanans' right to a clean and healthy environment.

The first Lindbergh-influenced phrase appears in the preamble, as follows:

"We the people of Montana grateful to God for the quiet beauty of our state, the grandeur of our mountains, the vastness of our rolling plains, and desiring to improve the quality of life, equality of opportunity and to secure the blessings of liberty for this and future generations do ordain and establish this constitution."

Article II's Declaration of Rights, in its Section 3 listing of Inalienable Rights, continues this theme. It declares that "all persons are born free and have certain inalienable rights. They include the right to a clean and healthful environment..."

Lindbergh, then seventy, appeared in Helena to give the third address in the Montana Constitutional Convention's distinguished speaker series. Newspapers across the state gave his remarks good play in their columns. This favorable press included an article headlined "Lindbergh urges control of land." Speaking to an informal evening meeting of convention delegates before his main address, Lindbergh said "government must be given supervision of natural resources, including land." Those controls were "bound to happen" if the trends toward environmental destruction were to be stopped, he said.

"The environment of the earth must be the property of the human species, not just a generation," he said.

He proposed a two-part approach to saving the environment. First, plans needed to be created. Second, there needed to be a mechanism for enforcing those plans.

"We must have the utmost freedom of use and control of our resources, but not to the extent that we destroy the environment for the future," he said.

Lindbergh said his flying career led to his involvement in ecology. Both as a civilian and military pilot, he became familiar with all areas of the world, and what he saw made him "highly alarmed at what was happening all over the earth."

He said Montana showed less evidence of environmental degradation than in many other places. He lauded the "great opportunity" for Montanans to protect the state's resources, but he refused to say "what should be done in the state," including passage of environmental laws.

Delegates heard Lindbergh reminisce about his introduction to Montana fifty years earlier. "I first flew here in 1922, barnstorming in Billings, Lewistown, and Red Lodge," he said, noting changes in the previous half-century. Subsequent visits to Montana allowed him to see "tremendous change. I see it more than you (residents) because each time I come here I compare what I see with what I have seen through the years."

Lindbergh told delegates that what they were doing was "where the hope lies. Supervision of the environment of the earth, or any section of it, can only be done satisfactorily by government, be it community, state, national or even international."

He emphasized that he was not advocating "one world" government, which he termed impractical. Yet "at the same time there must be universal cooperation on environment—it's bound to come." He called for "great judgment" on the part of governments when deciding on the limits to regulation and said he didn't consider industrialists an evil force bent on wrecking the earth.

"They have problems and need help; we must give that help to them."

Consistent with his dislike of excessive press coverage or overblown publicity, Lindbergh wouldn't allow television cameras in the meeting. He also refused a Helena radio station's request for a taped interview. Lindbergh did not, however, seem to mind delegates approaching to take snapshots of him. He autographed several photos.

One older delegate, Arnold Jacobson of Whitefish, shook hands with Lindbergh and said, "That's the second time I've met you. I shook your hand in 1926 in Butte, Montana."

Jacobson thought for a minute, then changed the year to 1927, when Lindbergh's cross-country tour in the *Spirit of St. Louis* brought him to Montana.

Present that night was one of Lindbergh's sons, Land. Land Lindbergh said his father visited his ranch near Missoula about once a year. He said he had "really good neighbors" who didn't make a fuss about him or his father.

During his time in Helena, Lindbergh heard and discussed issues having to do with the balance between economic development and environmental protection. That tension remains the subject of debate today.

Billings constitutional delegate Dave Drum (who along with three other Billings businessmen founded the Kampgrounds of America RV campground chain in 1962) asked Lindbergh how Montana could satisfy residents' desire for a clean environment as well as the need for job opportunities.

"There is no clear answer," Lindbergh said, noting the need for planning. "It is quite obvious that the human race cannot keep multiplying at the present rate."

"We've got to feel our way," but government enforcement of environmental-protection laws was essential, he said.

A lifetime of flying gave Lindbergh a global interest in and knowledge of conservation, but he spurned a simplistic approach to ensuring sustainability.

"It's a question of not simply conserving. It's a matter of conserving so we can use our natural resources," he said.

Existing generations should be able to do what they want so long as their actions don't pass on lasting damage to future generations, Lindbergh said.

He called for a multidisciplinary approach to environmental protection.

"All of our developments of civilized life, science, art, sociology—to be of value in the future—must rest on a sound environment."

Lindbergh was asked about possible overcrowding in Yellowstone and Glacier national parks, a trend that had magnified since his last public trip to Montana. He said more national parks were needed to lessen pressure on popular ones. Also, core areas of the parks should be off-limits to anyone but rangers so species of plants and animals most sensitive to human impact could survive, he said.

Humans may have to take on a different standard of living in the future, the flier said.

"It's very easy to adopt a false standard of living from the standpoint of material goods. We can be so affluent that the quality of life declines."

He said Montana Indians were in an enviable position, their quality of life being something the white society had barely if ever known.

Lindbergh's 1972 visit to Montana drew editorial praise from the Great Falls Tribune, which said he made a "great impression" at the convention. "Future generations of Montanans will be in debt to Lindbergh and to the convention delegates if the new constitution establishes the principal that each generation is the steward of the natural resources and should honor its obligations to coming generations."

Just before Lindbergh flew into Montana in 1972, his influence on the Treasure State's landscape was felt at a New York City function for East Coast movers and shakers. On February 3, 1972, Lindbergh was one of three people with ties to Montana who were hosts for a cocktail party at the Pierre Hotel attended by about 100 people. The purpose of the gathering was to shake cash from a so-called "money tree"—$150,000 was the goal—to help protect the integrity of Montana's 23,000-acre Lubrecht Experimental Forest, near Missoula. The forest was part of the University of Montana School of Forestry and was used and continues to be used as an outdoor laboratory and classroom.

A *New York Times* report published in the *Great Falls Tribune* described the fundraising project. Other party hosts were actress Myrna Loy and businessman Joseph E. McDowell. Loy was born Myrna Williams near Helena, and she said she agreed to serve "because I have Montana alumna privileges." McDowell was board chairman of Servomotion, a vending machine business. He lived in the state and was a UM trustee.

Lindbergh's appearance came two days before his seventieth birthday. He said was supporting the fundraiser "because it was absolutely essential" to maintain Lubrecht Forest intact. The flier circulated among guests with his wife, Anne, son Land, and Land's wife, Susan.

Party guests heard from Dr. Arnold Bolle, dean of the UM forestry school. He said the university acquired the forest in 1938 as a gift from the Anaconda

Company and the Northern Pacific Railroad. The forest was the largest watershed in the country under total academic control for research purposes, he said.

The problem, however, and the need for funds, arose from the fact that about 1,500 acres within or next to the forest, which were crucial to watershed studies, were not included in the gift. This included 640 acres that a Spokane land company had purchased four years earlier and resold by mail in small plots.

Remaining acreage not in university control was in private hands, and officials worried that it would end up being subdivided or sold in smaller plots.

Bolle said having even a small portion of the forest in private hands created the possibility that landowners might, wittingly or unwittingly, tamper with the delicate ecology of the entire forest. The checkerboard property ownership also increased the danger of fire, he said.

About 700 acres of private holdings had already passed into university ownership through its foundation or with the help of the Nature Conservancy, an organization that helps save endangered land in the public interest.

Bolle and Thomas J. Collins of the UM Foundation said Lubrecht Forest was especially valuable because it included all major forest types of the Northern Rockies. This made it ideal for a wide range of flora, fauna, and watershed studies.

The forest was not a designated wilderness area and was open to "responsible public use," the Times said. Fishermen and hunters used the forest regularly, roaming terrain that ranged from 3,700 to 6,850 feet. Vegetation included grassland, Ponderosa pine, Douglas fir, lodgepole pine, and western larch, with Engelmann spruce and alpine fir common at the highest elevations and most creek bottoms.

Bolle said the ultimate goal was to "develop a model of a Northern Rocky Mountain forest." Total control of the forest area would allow research into "many unsolved problems of timber growth and lumbering policy," he said.

Recalling the high society function fifty years later, Land Lindbergh said it was worthwhile even if the project goal wasn't totally accomplished.

"They didn't get all the property (that was sought), but it helped," he said, and at about the same time Montanans involved with the upcoming constitutional convention asked him to invite his father to speak at the event.

"I said I doubted very much that he would do it. As usual, he surprised me. He thought for a bit and said, 'I'll think about it,' " Land said.

"Then he said he would," which was in character for the man he called father, Land said.

"He usually avoided (public appearances) like the plague," but that he didn't this time was to Montana's benefit. The state constitutional convention gained input on environmental protection from not only the most famous flier in the world but also from someone who dedicated the later decades of his life to conservation efforts around the world.

TWENTY-TWO

Death at "my home"

Charles Augustus Lindbergh died on August 26, 1974. He was seventy-two. His death occurred about 3,200 miles away from the Montana city that played a key role in making him the most famous flier in the world.

News organizations around the world reported on Lindbergh's passing. Media coverage included his onetime home newspaper, the *Billings Gazette*, which published a United Press International dispatch atop the front page, above the flag, on August 27, 1974. Lindbergh died at an isolated beach cottage on the Hawaiian island of Maui. The death occurred forty-seven years after Lindbergh electrified the world with his daring solo flight from New York to Paris in the Spirit of St. Louis.

The world was reminded that the thirty-three-hour flight placed Lindbergh atop the pantheon of fliers because his was the first successful flight across the entire breadth of the Atlantic Ocean. His feat was compared to what Christopher Columbus had done in 1492 when he landed his ships in the West Indies, although the Italian explorer no longer is called the discoverer of America.

Lindbergh achieved fame in his day equivalent to, and perhaps surpassing that of, late twentieth-century and early twenty-first-century sports figures, athletes, musicians, and movie stars. Millions greeted his triumphant return to New York City from Europe aboard a ship sent to England by President Calvin Coolidge. A tour in the small plane that carried him across the Atlantic followed.

A torrent of news stories, newsreels, books, and public appearances made Lindbergh and his wife, Anne Morrow Lindbergh, the best-known couple in America —perhaps the world—in the 1930s.

Tragedy followed: Their first-born child, Charles, died in a bungled kidnapping. Controversy dogged Lindbergh, too: He tangled with President Franklin Roosevelt, first in 1934 over what Lindbergh considered FDR's mistaken and deadly decision to have Army pilots take over air mail delivery and then in 1941 on the issue of whether the United States should go to war against Nazi Germany and its ally, Mussolini's fascist regime in Italy.

Yet little of that mattered when Lindbergh's end came. He died from cancer, a malignant tumor, bathed in the privacy he sought nearly his entire adult life. He had been released from a New York hospital in July 1974 and went to Hawaii to spend his final days.

Anne Lindbergh and their son Land, were with him when he died. He lapsed into unconsciousness at 9 p.m. on Sunday, August 25, but his physician, Dr. Milton Howell, said he been alert and aware of his surroundings until then.

Howell said Lindbergh spent the last days of his life planning his own funeral. He was buried in work clothes in a wooden coffin "made by local cowboys," and his funeral was a simple private ceremony.

Lindbergh had been treated for several weeks at Columbia-Presbyterian Medical Center in New York City. He was taken secretly to Maui a week before his death. Told he could go to his Connecticut home to die,

Lindbergh said he wanted to return to Maui instead.

"That is my home," he said.

Lindbergh was flown to Hawaii on a stretcher. All that could be done for him in New York had been done, his doctor said.

The Little Falls, Minnesota, native had arranged for a small cottage by the ocean as his home. It was located on the southern tip of Maui, where the Lindberghs had resided for several years.

The *Gazette* account included this paragraph summarizing Lindbergh's impact on aviation:

"By making the first solo flight over a vast ocean, Lindbergh helped to prepare public acceptance of the change in air flight from a limited, experimental science, appealing mainly to daredevils and thrill seekers, to the present booming industry which provides transportation for millions."

Twenty-three
Still a Montana presence

One part of Lindbergh's legacy in Billings is that a major street, North 27th, was named for him soon after his 1927 trans-Atlantic flight. North 27th, which runs from Montana Avenue to Billings Logan International Airport, became Lindbergh Boulevard for several years.

The author's research failed to find the exact date when the City Council made the street-naming decision. Nor is it clear from sketchy records when the arterial reverted to its previous name—or whether it officially ever has.

Billings Gazette digital archives include a September 30, 1938, reference to Lindbergh Boulevard. The paper's readers were told it had become possible to drive a loop from downtown to Exposition Avenue, next to the fairgrounds, then up Black Otter Trail to the airport and back downtown on Lindbergh Boulevard.

After that, the *Gazette* contains no further mention of Lindbergh Boulevard until 1969, with a further reference in 1981—and that's a nostalgia piece about a veteran city councilman and longtime Billings resident who wanted to bring the name back.

On January 30, 1981, the *Gazette* published a short item headlined "Great idea, but." The paper complimented Councilman Mike Kennedy for his proposal to rename North 27th to the name it once had honoring "Lucky Lindy." (Right there, the *Gazette* showed some ignorance of Billings history because Lindbergh was known as "Slim" during his time in the Magic City; the "Lucky" part of his nickname was added later by national media to describe Lindbergh's survival from several brushes with death as an air mail pilot.)

"The only trouble with the change would be that most people would continue to call it 'Airport Road' or '27th Street'—just like many still refer to Broadway as North 28th, or a shortening to Lindy Lane," the Gazette said.

Perhaps someone on the paper's staff dug through microfilm and found a December 20, 1969, article. Its headline was "Lindbergh Lane Around Here?" Former mayor Howard Hultgren was quoted as saying that interesting, long-forgotten facts sometimes appeared in old, dry city traffic studies.

A "real stumper" from the traffic studies, he said, is Lindbergh Lane.

"Try to find that one on a city map. It's North 27th Street, renamed by the city council following Charles Lindbergh's spectacular-at-the-time solo flight across the Atlantic Ocean."

To make matters more interesting, Hultgren said he was unaware of any city council action to rescind its hero-worship vote. Thus, the official name of North 27th, at least in 1969, may still have been Lindbergh Lane. Or, it may be Lindbergh Lane now.

A further curious item appeared in the *Gazette* weather section on October 18, 1999. The report of state extreme temperatures said the overnight low was eleven degrees at White Sulphur Springs—and the high was seventy-two at Lindbergh Lane.

Echoes of Lindbergh's presence in Montana lingered into the 1980s, the 1990s, and even into the first decades of the twenty-first century.

For example, in the fall of 1987, a Montana author, who also was a small-plane pilot, took off in an old Cessna Cardinal to tour the country. Michael Parfit, who then lived in the western Montana town of St.

Ignatius, embarked on a trip that took him to eighteen US. cities. He used the tour to promote the book he had written, just set to hit bookstores, titled Chasing the Glory.

The book chronicled the 25,000-mile air journey Parfit had taken a year earlier, following the route across America that Lindbergh flew in his 1927 tour to promote commercial aviation after his trans-Atlantic flight in May of that year.

"In the summer of 1927, Charles Lindbergh came home from Paris, hero of the world, and made a tour of the 48 United States to praise the business and machinery of flight," Parfit wrote.

"He landed in every state, spent time in 82 cities, and flew over about 200 more," Parfit wrote. Lindbergh landed in two Montana cities, Butte and Helena, and he flew over three more: Billings, his base for the three months in 1922 when he was a wing walker and parachute jumper, part of a barnstorming outfit, Missoula, and Great Falls.

Parfit left Montana in February 1987 and spent nearly six months flying over valleys, rivers, farms, mountains, and towns along Lindbergh's 1927 route, gathering material for his book.

"It felt a little like I was going on something like the Oregon Trail," Parfit said.

In his book, Parfit summarizes his retracing of Lindbergh's trip: "The route was old but fresh. On the map of the United States, the line of his flight turned and twisted and doubled back. He flew everywhere, saw everything, spent hour after hour in the air."

Parfit's book drew acclaim from the Charles A. Lindbergh Fund in Minneapolis, which awarded him a commemorative medal.

In July 1988, just before the Big Sky International Airshow started, *Gazette* reporter John Firehammer reviewed the Magic City's rich aviation history. His article included what, in 1913, was Montana's longest air flight, from Billings to Laurel to Park City and back again, a trip in a Curtiss biplane made by local dentist Dr. Frank Bell. Then came Lindbergh in 1922, although he had not yet solo piloted a plane when he came to town, and the Minnesotan renewed his ties to Billings in 1927 when, as the world-famous trans-Atlantic flier, he circled the city and dropped a note to residents that landed on a downtown street.

Billings' current airport came into existence in 1929, and notables who stopped there included Amelia Earhart and Will Rogers in the early and mid-1930s, then Lindbergh in 1939.

Rogers showed the humor he was famed for when, after landing at the airport, he reportedly was met by a boy on a black horse. Rogers saw the horse, popped his head out of the cockpit and, knowing he had landed on the Rimrocks, sandstone cliffs that rise 400 feet above the city, asked the boy, "Is that my transportation up town?"

Residents of Billings and its sprawling trade area again were reminded of Lindbergh's time in the city in 1992 when Edward W. Kraske died. His obituary included a paragraph that recalled the memorable event from his teenage days seventy years earlier:

"One of his fondest boyhood memories was in 1922 when Charles Lindbergh spent three days at the Kraske family farm in Worden when on his way to St. Louis."

One of Kraske's sons, Bill, a Billings resident, said in 2022 that his father's nickname was "Steady Eddy" because "he was always on the move." The moniker signaled a lifetime of accomplishments that went beyond befriending a wing walker and parachute jumper who was a few years older than he. The senior Kraske, born in Laurel, had moved to Huntley Project with his parents in 1911. After graduating from the National Electrical and Automotive School in Los Angeles, he operated the first electrical utility on the project, owned and managed the Project Locker Plant in Worden, with branch meat lockers in Custer and Huntley, for forty-eight years, and owned and operated the Project Theater in Worden until he sold it in 1958. Ed Kraske also maintained rental properties in Billings and Worden.

Great Falls residents learned in 1998 that someone closely involved with Lindbergh's family was living in their city. That was Jean Saunders, who worked as a private secretary for Lindbergh and his wife, Anne, from 1957 until 1975, a year after Charles died. Her service occurred at the Lindbergh's home in Darien, Connecticut. Saunders and her husband, Allen, later moved to Montana.

Saunders said the family's desire for privacy, shaped by decades of mammoth press attention and publicity seekers following their every move, made her uneasy.

"Charles Lindbergh still casts a long shadow, even though he's been dead for twenty years," Saunders said. She contrasted Lindbergh, who flew across the Atlantic solo, without a radio in his plane, with astronauts whom schoolchildren were much better acquainted with and who had become modern heroes—especially Neil Armstrong and Buzz Aldrin, the first men to walk on the moon, their July 1969 achievement the culmination of a big-budget, NASA-backed project.

Saunders began working for the Lindberghs a quarter-century after their first-born child, Charles Jr., was kidnapped and killed, a 1932 event that captured worldwide newspaper coverage and was labeled "The Crime of the Century."

Saunders praised Charles and Anne for the grace they displayed when they found their infant son had been kidnapped, the wait before his body was found, and through a trial in New Jersey that riveted the nation's and attention, not to mention the years that followed.

"It was a terrible ordeal, and they handled it so beautifully," she said. During her employment with the Lindberghs, she rarely heard them talk about the kidnapping, even to their five surviving children who grew to adulthood.

Saunders heard or saw first hand times when Charles Lindbergh used challenging situations that his children found themselves in to impart life lessons. The practicality and problem-solving shown there probably were key factors in his ability to fly millions of miles all over the globe for many years without a serious mishap. In fact, "his idea of a pilot's checklist, which does not leave safety to second chance, is now second nature to pilots."

Yet Lindbergh's admiration for machines and aviation technology made him susceptible to a political blind spot as U.S. entry into World War II loomed from 1939 until 1941, before Japan's December 7, 1941, attack on Pearl Harbor plunged the country into combat.

Lindbergh admired the "disciplined minds" of German military officials, including Hermann Göring, Adolf Hitler's second-in-command and head of the Luftwaffe, after he toured Nazi aircraft facilities in the mid- and late 1930s, Saunders said. "He did not admire the Nazis."

She completed her job with the Lindberghs in 1975, her final task being to sort through thousands of condolence cards sent to Anne after Charles' death. When the Tribune article was published, Anne was still alive in New England but frail at age ninety-two. She died a year later at ninety-three.

A new generation of Montanans, twenty-first-century readers of the *Billings Gazette*, learned of Charles's Lindbergh's ties to Billings in the new millennium—if they didn't already know. On March 8, 2007, the *Gazette* published an obituary of Livingston resident Harold Alton Shanstrom, who died four days earlier in Helena at age ninety-nine. Shanstrom, father of retired U.S. District Judge Jack Shanstrom (who spent years on the federal bench in Billings), was born in 1908 in Nassau, Minnesota. He played baritone in his high school band, which greeted Lindbergh at Little Falls, Minnesota, when he made a triumphant return to his boyhood hometown after he flew across the Atlantic in May 1927, according to the obituary.

Also in March 2007, *Gazette* readers read about the recent trans-Atlantic flight of the Airbus A-380, a trip intended to market the plane's potential in the United States. "Airplanes have dramatically changed since Charles Lindbergh's ground-breaking flight on the *Spirit of St. Louis* in 1927," the paper said, continuing:

"The Airbus A380 is faster, roomier and more powerful than its historic counterpart." Lufthansa AG and Airbus used the flight to show off the superjumbo jet to potential U.S. buyers and airports, which the companies hoped would become flight bases.

The article included a graphic that compared the Airbus and Lindbergh's Ryan Airlines-manufactured plane. Here are the specifications of the Airbus 380 and the *Spirit of St. Louis*:

	Airbus A380	Spirit of St. Louis
Length	239 feet, 3 inches	27 feet, 8 inches
Height	79 feet, 7 inches	9 feet, 8 inches
Wingspan	261 feet, 8 inches	46 feet
Weight	617.3 tons	2.5 tons
Passengers	Up to 550 passengers; 28 crew	1 pilot
Range	8,000 nautical miles	4,000 nautical miles
Fuel capacity	81,890 gallons	450 gallons

Further commentary on Lindbergh's flying ability came on May 20, 2007—eighty years to the day after he took off from Roosevelt Field on Long Island—in the form of a newspaper article written by Charles A. Thornsvard, a Billings physician and commercial-rated pilot. He reviewed Lindbergh's flying record in the four years 1923 to 1926, before his fabled flight. He had made 7,189 flights and logged 1,790 flight hours. In 1925, he graduated first in his cadet class at the Army Air Service flight school at Kelly Field in Texas, earning him qualification as a "pursuit" or fighter pilot. He had survived a training gauntlet that saw 104 prospective pilots start training in 1924—and only nineteen graduate.

"No, it was not a fool who took wing that day, who flew alone while fighting oppressive sleepiness and struggling through storms and hours of instrument flight with just compass, needle ball, altimeter, and airspeed indicator. It was a pilot," Thornsvard wrote.

Drawing from Lindbergh's book The Autobiography of Values, Thornsvard said Lindbergh had learned that "fear could be managed by a balance between the intellect and instinct. He thought he could do it. And he did."

Thornsvard drew an incident from the book that illustrated Lindbergh's character. It occurred in the fall of 1922, when Lindbergh was getting ready to leave Billings and return to Lincoln. He related a conversation he had with a fellow aviator before departing.

" 'Why don't you take that girl in the tent show along with you?' the aviator said. 'She'd go if you invited her. She's just the kind for a trip like that,' " Lindbergh recalled, but he resisted the idea.

"It would hardly have occurred to me, and it certainly would not have suited me," he wrote.

A year later, a New York City woman whose great-grandfather employed Charles Lindbergh as a mechanic at his Billings garage brought her musical talent to Billings. Lee Ann Westover, lead vocalist in the Lascivious Biddies, a "cocktail pop" group, and the other three group members sang at the Alberta Bair Theater in May 2008.

Westover said that while going through her grandfather's belongings in Florida after he died a few years earlier, she found an old *Gazette* article about his father, Bob Westover, and his employee in 1922, Charles Lindbergh.

A few months after Lee Ann Westover took home a copy of the clipping about the great-grandfather she never met, her Billings show at the ABT was booked.

"I just can't wait to see Billings," she said just before her group's gig in the city. "This is just crazy to think there's a little part of my gene pool there."

The December 14, 1958, *Gazette* article she found told how Bob Westover came to Billings in 1911, set himself up as one of the city's first auto mechanics, learned to fly, got an airplane, and barnstormed in Montana and Wyoming in the early years of the decade with Lindbergh and others.

Here is what thrilled Lee Ann when she read it in the article about her ancestor:

"Westover gunned the fragile plane low over a small town, with the town residents gaping. Lindbergh would bail out by parachute. Westover would then land in a nearby field and wait for business." Those willing to go up in a contraption many were seeing for the first time in their life paid ten dollars each for a short ride.

Lee Ann said that reading about her ancestor gave her insight into her own personality.

"For most of my life, I always felt like a weirdo, a black sheep. 'Oh, she's always doing something odd like running off to New York to make it in show business.' He was the first clue that there was a wild streak in my family. It helped me feel a little more at one with my family," she said.

TWENTY-FOUR

Echoes of the kidnapping in Montana

Montanans got another reminder of Lindbergh's life, with a direct connection to the Treasure State, in 2014. That was when a story with the attention-grabbing headline "Key player in Lindbergh baby kidnapping told his story in letter to Montana newspaper" was published in Missoula and Butte.

Here's how the December 1, 2014, article, reprinted in the *Montana Standard*, begins:

"The envelope, yellowed with age, is addressed to 'Editor of Missoulian, Missoula, Montana.'

"Folded inside is a half-page note and a four-page letter written on ledger paper from the Dayton State Bank of Montana and signed 'John F. Condon (Jafsie).'

" 'If you can use this, you are welcome to it,'" Condon wrote in the note. "'If not, no harm done.'"

Who was "Jafsie"? That was another name for John F. Condon who was a major figure in the attempted ransom for Charles Lindbergh Jr., the twenty-month-old son of Charles and Anne Lindbergh after the toddler was kidnapped from their New Jersey home in 1932.

Condon wrote a book, Jafsie Tells All, in 1936 that described how he tried to help Lindbergh deliver $50,000 in ransom money in exchange for the safe return of his son.

Missoula resident Michael Peretti found the letter in 2014 while cleaning a drawer in his Missoula home. Since the letter was addressed to the *Missoulian* editor, he decided to see if the newspaper's then editor, Sherry Devlin, was interested in it.

"I knew I had it, but I guess I had forgotten about it," Peretti said. "My grandfather had a small file cabinet and he'd throw in coins and things he thought might be valuable."

Peretti's grandfather, Don Hacker, gave Peretti the cabinet in the 1970s when Hacker was moving his office from Lakeside, a town along Flathead Lake. The bequest from his grandfather included "a whole bunch of antique pistols," said Peretti, who thinks he was twenty-three at the time.

In the collection was a small, 33-caliber revolver, which Don Hacker said was the weapon that Condon carried when he accompanied Lindbergh to the site of the failed ransom exchange.

In his book, however, Condon claimed that Lindbergh carried the pistol that night. Condon was worried that Lindbergh might use the gun and was relieved when the pilot agreed to stay in the waiting car.

Peretti said he didn't know about the Lindbergh kidnapping until his grandfather showed him the pistol and told him about its connection to the crime.

Peretti's connection to Condon arose from his great-uncle, Ralph Hacker, a New York architect married to Condon's daughter, Myra. Ralph Hacker and Don's brother, Fred, ran the Dayton bank.

Condon wrote the letter to the *Missoulian* during a visit to the Hackers in Dayton more than five years after the kidnapping. Peretti saw no indication that Condon mailed the letter, which had no stamp or postmark.

Condon's letter didn't mention the *Missoulian's* editor in 1937, Warren Davis, but it said the paper's news chief was "the only editor who gave a true account of how I handed the money to the kidnapper." Condon claimed at the 1935 trial of Bruno Richard Hauptmann, who was convicted of the kidnapping and death, and executed in the electric chair, and in his book, that he was face-to-face with Hauptmann on April 2, 1932. Condon said he handed over Lindbergh's money to Hauptmann, then learned that the German-born carpenter had given back a note with vague information about where the baby could be found.

Speaking to Condon after the encounter, Lindbergh reportedly said, "Doctor, we've been double-crossed." Condon's account was disputed by Hauptmann's defense team and others. They said the ransom money had been thrown over a Bronx cemetery wall and thus Condon couldn't have identified Hauptmann as the recipient.

Condon's belief that he could get a fair shake in the *Missoulian* apparently stemmed from a short article that appeared in that paper and in the *Helena Independent-Record* in late August 1937. Dated Kalispell (the largest town close to Dayton), the article said Condon, "in this district on an extended vacation," rebutted statements that he threw the ransom money over a wall.

"I handed him (Hauptmann) the packet containing the money and he, in turn, with his other hand, handed me a note," Condon said.

Condon said he didn't throw the ransom money "over any wall like a coward."

This is one more mystery about the kidnapping, which has spawned conspiracy theories that persist to this day.

Conclusion

Charles Lindbergh was a hero, and he remains a hero now, almost fifty years after his death. He was, and is, as much a hero in Montana as anywhere else in the United States or in the world. Yet, he was a flawed one, as most if not all heroes are.

To illustrate this, one need only point to Lindbergh's blind spot to the rise of Adolf Hitler and Nazism in the years before World War II. Yet to call him a neo-Nazi, as some did then and some still do today, seems beyond reason. Yes, he was politically naive and made ugly statements, most notably in a speech in Des Moines in September 1941. Was that due to his traits as an engineer, a genius in that field, and someone not educated or trained in the subtleties and shifting tides of politics?

And if Lindbergh were a true Nazi sympathizer in his thirties, what does that make people like Montana's Democratic Senator Burton Wheeler and future Billings mayor Willard Fraser, who also were America Firsters? Do they pick up the neo-Nazi label, too, in a case of guilt by association?

Furthermore, what about Montana's Jeanette Rankin, the first women elected to Congress in 1916? She, along with many others in Congress, voted against U.S. entry into World War I, then called the Great War. Then, consistent with her belief that young men were sent to war by old men thumping their chests, she cast the lone vote against declaring war on Japan after the Pearl Harbor attack.

It seems much wiser to look at the totality of Lindbergh's life, including his influence to this day in Montana. His 1927 "goodwill tour," which brought him to the Treasure State for stops in Butte and Helena plus flyovers of Billings, Great Falls, and Missoula, undoubtedly contributed to an atmosphere of support for commercial aviation in the state. That led to the construction of major airports in Billings, Butte, Great Falls, Kalispell, and Missoula, plus in Gallatin County, the location of Bozeman Yellowstone International Airport, the state's busiest.

Of at least equal importance, Montana for fifty years has had a state constitution renowned for its environmental protection. The drafting of this landmark document, approved by the state constitutional convention in 1972 and ratified that year by Montana voters, would have happened with or without Lindbergh. But if he had not addressed convention delegates in February 1972 and urged them to include conservation wording in the constitution, would those key provisions have become part of Montana's legal landscape?

"A hero is someone who has given his or her life to something bigger than one's self," according to Joseph Campbell, the leading scholar of the role of myth and heroes in societies from antiquity to now.

Campbell asserted that there are two types of deeds that heroes accomplish: "physical ... in which the hero performs a courageous act in battle or saves a life" and "spiritual...in which the hero learns to experience the supernormal range of human spiritual life and then comes back with a message."

All one needs to do is read Lindbergh's Pulitzer Prize-winning 1954 book, *The Spirit of St. Louis*, to see that he experienced spirituality in May 1927 when, as a twenty-five-year-old, he flew alone, without a radio, with primitive maps, in cloud banks, more than 3,000 miles across the Atlantic. As he skimmed the ocean, sometimes less than 50 feet above the water, sleep-deprived and fending off what would have been a fatal urge to close his eyes a bit, he came as close to sensing the presence of someone or something bigger than himself as any human can.

When he was in the twenty-third hour of his thirty-three-and-a-half hour, sleep-deprived flight from New York to Paris, Lindbergh said he became aware of "ghostly presences—vaguely outlined forms, transparent, moving, riding weightless with me in the plane." He said he wasn't surprised at their coming and, without turning his head, he could see them "as clearly as though in my normal field of vision."

What he called "phantoms" spoke with friendly human voices. They had no body, yet he sensed they were "human in outline form—emanations from the experience of ages, inhabitants of a universe closed to mortal men." Lindbergh felt himself to be on the borderline of known life and "a greater realm beyond, as though caught in the field of gravitation between two planets, acted on by forces I can't control, forces too weak to be measured by any means at my command, yet representing powers incomparably stronger than I've known."

His spiritual deeds combined with the very definite physical manifestation that Montanans saw make Charles Lindbergh an unchallenged hero in the Montana he first got to know in August 1922. When he flew into Hardin and Billings, Jack Lynch and Banty Rogers made up his tiny circle of familiar faces in the Treasure State. Now, though, all Montanans can claim him as one of their own.

Photos
General

Portrait of Charles Lindbergh in pilot gear. Photo taken between 1925 and 1935. Montana Historical Research Center Photograph Archives, Helena, Montana.

Charles Lindbergh with an undentified woman, believed to be his mother, Evangeline Lodge Land. Montana Historical Research Center Photograph Archives, Helena, Montana

Billings 1922

"Daredevil Slim"(in center, with lettering on the back of his jacket), as Charles Lindbergh was known in Billings, at a local air strip in 1922. Lindbergh hadn't yet piloted a plane but came to Montana as a 20-year-old parachute jumper and wing walker who performed in exhibitions given by a Lincoln, Nebraska barnstorming group. Courtesy Western Heritage Center, Billings, Montana.

Cropped version of the above photo, showing Lindbergh in greater detail. Courtesy Western Heritage Center, Billings, Montana.

LINDBERGH IN MONTANA • 195

The Westover Garage on the 2300 block of First Avenue North in Billings, as it appeared in the 1920s when brothers Bob and Ed Westover owned the business. When his barnstorming ended in Billings, Charles Lindbergh worked here for several weeks as a car and engine mechanic. Courtesy Western Heritage Center, Billings, Montana

The porcelein water jug that Charles Lindbergh carried on his boat for his ill-fated journey down the Yellowstone River in October 1922. He gave the jug to Ed Kraske and his siblings, and it has been in the possession of the Kraske family for the past century. Dennis Gaub

1927 visit to Montana-Butte

Lindbergh's pending arrival in Butte prompted businesses to display messages welcoming him, including this photograph of him and an "Ace of Hearts" sign, at the Maytag Shop, 126 West Broadway Street .Butte-Silver Bow Public Archives, Smithers.04.021.04

A huge crowd awaited Lindbergh's arrival from Boise. Photo depicts the throng surrounding the stage and in bleachers waiting to greet him. The banner on stage reads, "We love Lindbergh." Butte-Silver Bow Public Archives, Smithers.22.070.01

LINDBERGH IN MONTANA • 197

The Spirit of St. Louis parked in front of the Butte National Airport. Butte-Silver Bow Public Archives. Smithers.22.071.01

Charles Lindbergh and Butte men standing near Lindbergh's airplan after he arrived in the Mining City. Butte-Silver Bow Archives, Smithers.32.028.03-.07

Charles Lindbergh wearing pilot's clothing standing with two men at the airport in Butte. The Spirit of St. Louis is in the background. Butte-Silver Bow Public Archives, Smithers.32.028.08

Charles Lindbergh fishing from a canoe at what was then Elbow Lake. It was renamed Lindbergh Lake in 1928. His getaway to an idyllic Swan River Valley location, the only vacation he got during his nationwide "goodwill tour," was organized by Butte and Missoula businessmen. Montana Historical Society Research Center Photograph Archives, Helena, Montana.

LINDBERGH IN MONTANA • 199

1927 visit to Montana - Helena

Charles Lindbergh next to his plane soon after landing in Montana's capital city. Montana Historical Society Research Center Photograph Archives, Helena, Montana.

Spirit of St. Louis parked at the Helena Municipal Airport. Montana Historical Society Research Center Photograph Archives, Helena, Montana.

Charles Lindbergh, in pilot gear, standing in front of his plane after landing in Helena. Montana Historical Society Research Center Photograph Archives, Helena, Monrana..

Lindbergh being greeted by dignitaries upon his arrival in Helena. Montana Hisorical Society Research Center Photograph Archives, Helena, Monrana.

LINDBERGH IN MONTANA • 201

Charles Lindbergh stands as he gets an open air reception in a Helena parade during the Montana State Fair. Montana Historical Society Researech Centrer Photo Archives, Helena, Montana.

Charles Lindbergh sitting in an automobile, flanked by Governor John Erickson and Mayor Percy Witmer. Montana Historical Society Research Centrer Photograph Archives, Helena, Montana.

Lindbergh landmarks in Montana

Lindbergh Lake, in the Swan River Valley, today. Google Earth

Lubrecht Forest, west of Missoula. Charles and Anne Morrow Lindbergh helped preseerve the integrity of the forest by playing host to a high-society party in New York City in 1972. Dennis Gaub

LINDBERGH IN MONTANA • 203

Northeast corner of Homestead Business Park, at King Avenue West and 20th Street West, in Billings. This major business center was several miles west of the city's core in 1922 and was where Ben Hogan farmed and provided an airstrip for early pilots, including Jack Lynch and Bob Westover, whose planes took Charles Lindbergh skyward. Dennis Gaub

Westover Garage site today. The building was demolished in the spring of 2022. Besides the Westover business, over the years it housed several car dealerships, a grocery store and, into the early 1990s, a used camera store. Dennis Gaub

Clark Park in Butte today. When Charles Lindbergh stopped in Butte in 1927, at least 10,000 people crowded into the park to see him. Butte, at that time the largest city between Minneapolis and Seattle, had about 100,000 people who lived within the Mining City and in surrounding mining camps. Today, Butte's population is about 34,500. Dennis Gaub

Bill Roberts Golf Course in Helena today. Charles Lindbergh landed here in September 1927. Google Earth

Acknowledgements

The genesis of this book can be traced to a visit I made in December 2019 to the Huntley Project Homesteader Museum in Worden, Montana. I had just relocated to Billings, Montana, my professional base for most of my 45 years in the everyday working world. Fresh from being steeped in World War II military aviation history — my second book, *Midway Bravery*, had been published six months earlier — I was fleshing out the skeleton for what became my third book.

Over the years, I had heard bits and pieces of stories about one of Billings' most famous residents, Charles Lindbergh. Somewhere, I had learned that he had a chance meeting with members of a Huntley Project farm family in October 1922. This happened when he abandoned his idea to float down the Yellowstone and Missouri rivers back to St. Louis after his 1922 barnstorming foray into Montana. He had displayed his wing walking and parachute jumping skills to audiences in Billings, Lewistown and other towns in central Montana, and it was time for him to get serious about becoming an airplane pilot.

So, on one mild early winter afternoon, I drove 30 miles or so east to the museum, thinking there had to be a book in that story. It didn't happen immediately, though, even after I saw the homesteader museum exhibit depicting the interaction between a 20-year-old Lindbergh and a 14-year-old E.W. "Ed" Kraske, whose younger brothers and cousins also got to meet the young Minnesotan. That story somehow inspired my first venture into serious fiction since about my junior year at Billings West High School, when I took an English composition class. After that, my professional writing became focused on nonfiction, first as a reporter for the Billings Gazette and three other newspapers, then as a business writer for two software companies. Yet, the creative juices were still flowing and they enabled me to pen *Sky Dreamer*.

Lindbergh's time in Montana, however, was an idea for a book that wouldn't go away, so as *Sky Dreamer* approached reality, I started researching what became this book.

One of the first, and still finest, experiences in this project came on a glorious day in June 2022 when my wife, Cathie, and I drove with Billings resident Bill Kraske to what had been his family's farm along the Yellowstone River in the Worden area. This is the spot where Bill's father, Ed Kraske, saw Lindbergh poling his $2 boat down the river. And it's where the Kraske family befriended Lindbergh after he gave up the idea of a water trip back to the Midwest to finish learning to fly. Instead, the Kraskes gave Lindbergh a wagon ride to a nearby station where he boarded a train back to Billings, then took another train to Lincoln, Nebraska. A few months later, Lindbergh got his first plane, a used, World War I surplus Curtiss "Jenny," learned to fly it, and he was on the path toward becoming the most famous person in the world.

Bill, thank you! And special thanks to your sister, Jean Gabel, for her hospitality last August (2022). Cathie and I spent a delightful afternoon at Jean's home, and she allowed me to photograph the white water jug that Lindbergh was carrying 100 years ago and which he gave to their father. (Bill was the youngest child of Ed

Kraske, and Jean the oldest. I haven't met their brother, Gary, who lives on the East Coast.)

My gratitude also extends to the Montana Historical Society's splendid archives department in Helena, in particular Jeff Malcomson, head of the photo archives section, and Heather Hultman, a staffer there. Jeff and Heather helped me locate photos of Lindbergh's visit to Helena in September 1927. Thanks! Likewise, Lindsay Mulcahy, with the Butte-Silver Bow Archives in Montana's Mining City, steered me in the right direction there to find photos and newspaper clips that enhanced the narrative.

It's been especially rewarding to chat on the phone with Land Lindbergh, second-oldest child of Charles and Anne Morrow Lindbergh. Land, now retired, has been a respected Western Montana rancher for more than a half-century, and his recollections of when his father came to Montana to speak at the 1972 state constitutional convention were especially valuable.

Kevin Koustra, executive director of the Western Heritage Center in Billings, furnished two valuable photos depicting Lindbergh's time in the Magic City in 1922.

A bonus interaction occurred this summer when *Helena Independent-Record* editor Phil Drake contacted me and asked me to write an article about Lindbergh's visit to the capital city. The article, timed to coincide with the 95th anniversary of the 1927 event, appeared in the September 4, 2022, issue of the IR and also in at least three other Lee Enterprise papers in Montana, the *Billings Gazette*, the *Montana Standard* in Butte, and the *Missoulian* in Missoula. It's hard to measure the value of publicity like that, but it's much appreciated.

To my editor, Craig Lancaster, this is the fourth

"rodeo," the fourth book we've been on together. Thanks to a fellow ink-stained wretch who's found writing success outside the Fourth Estate.

And to Cathie, who I married in March 2021. You patiently read an electronic copy of the manuscript for this book, pointing out both typos and clunky, unclear wording. This author has been made better from the support of his partner. All my love, sweetie!

Sources

Introduction
6 "a fox terrier named Booster…" *Lindbergh*, A. Scott Berg, 1998
7 "banners advertising the garage …" *Billings Gazette*, August 2, 1931

Chapter 1-The life of a flier begins
14 "A newspaper advertisement invited readers …" *Nebraska State Journal*, May 9, 1920
14 "Passenger flights will be given" *Nebraska State Journal*, May 9, 1920
14 another newspaper ad, *Lincoln Star Journal*, September 8, 1920
16 "worked for the NAC for a year and a half" *Lincoln Star*, May 6, 1921
17 "especially the aircraft business," *Nebraska State Journal*, Lincoln, June 25, 1922

Chapter 2-Lindbergh's first flight
19 "had during the just-ended Great War …" *Montana and the Sky*, Frank W. Wiley, Holden Printing Company, 1966
21 "with the laced end hanging down …" *We*, Grosset & Dunlap, published by arrangement with G.P Putnam's Sons, 1927
23 "banning all forms of stunt flying …" *Chicago Tribune*, July 4, 1922
24 stunt flier at Pine Valley, Camden, NJ, *Morning Post*, July 6, 1929

Chapter 3-Heading to Montana
27 A local newspaper account, *Lamar*, CO, *Register*, August 2, 1922

28 The barnstormers were performing, *Anaconda Standard*, September 4, 1927

29 By then, Lynch had finished, *We*

30 "We had the plane in shape by then," *Anaconda Standard*, September 4, 1927

30 The buzz started, *Billings Gazette*, August 16, 1922

Chapter 4-Treasure State Thrills

33 Furthermore, the barnstormers performed in Hardin, *Hardin Tribune*, August 22, 1922

34 People in Hardin may have wondered, *Hardin Tribune*, August 25, 1922

35 Lynch gave an example of the hand-to-mouth existence, *Anaconda Standard*, September 4, 1927

36 Lynch used this approach, *Billings Gazette*, August 27, 1922

37 Bob Westover recalled a near-death, *Billings Gazette*, June 19, 1927

38 "Slim was the quickest guy to leave a ship," Billings Gazette, May 24, 1927

38 On one Sunday afternoon in late August 1922, *Billings Gazette*, August 28, 1922

Chapter 5-Flying at the fairs

41 The Midland Empire Fair opened, *Billings Gazette*, September 20, 1922

41 The seventh annual Midland Empire fair drew a record, *Billings Gazette*, September 23, 1922

42 "At Billings ... our field," *We*

42 In 1931, four years after Lindbergh, *Billings Gazette*, August 2, 1931

43 One was Billings resident Phil Scala, Facebook post, May 2022

43   Not everyone in Billings held fond memories, Joyce M. Jensen, *Pieces and Places of Billings History: Local Markers and Sites*, Western Heritage Press, 1994

44   Jensen, elaborating in 2022, Joyce Jensen, June 12, 2022, phone interview

45   "At the Lewistown fair," *We*

45   "Perfect weather" helped the fair, *Great Falls Tribune*, October 7, 1922

46   The younger Riddick joined the Army Air Service, *Missoulian*, May 20, 2019

46   Born in Madison, Wisconsin, *Missoulian*, June 18, 1979

46   In the summer of 1919, he began, *Washington Times*, March 30, 1922

46   A Rochester newspaper account, *Rochester, NY, Democrat and Chronicle*, November 13, 1938

Chapter 6-Boating the Yellowstone River
49   Lindbergh bought a small boat, *We*
50   As recounted almost forty years later, *Billings Gazette*, November 5, 1961

Chapter 7-A plane of his own
56   Lindbergh missed the real bargain days, *We*
56   "One of the interesting facts," *We*
58   He did, however, have the advantage, *We*
58   When Lindbergh left for Americus, *Lindbergh* (Berg)
60   "Landing fields are of primary importance," *We*

Chapter 8-Flying with Father
64   The June 1923 incident gained notice, *Minneapolis Star*, June 6, 1923

Chapter 9-The break he needed

68 In the evening after taking up, *We*
70 He and a companion filled a car, *We*
71 December 1923 found Lindbergh barnstorming, Berg
72 The senior Lindbergh was in a coma, *Minneapolis Star*, May 26, 1924

Chapter 10-Flying the mail

75 Readers were told that he was the only man, *St. Louis Globe-Democrat*, July 3, 1925
76 That purportedly resulted in a reduction, *St. Louis Post-Dispatch*, June 18, 1926
78 They heard the drone of Lindbergh's plane, *Oshkosh, Wisconsin, Northwestern*, September 17, 1926
79 Less than two months, *Aston, Illinois, Evening Telegram*, November 4, 1926
80 Lindbergh left Maywood Field, *St. Louis Globe-Democrat*, January 15, 1927
80 For example, the newspaper in the Montana city, *Billings Gazette*, January 31, 1927

Chapter 11-The Atlantic beckons

82 "I thought of him a lot" *Billings Gazette*, August 2, 1931
83 In the spring of 1927, seemingly all Billings, *Billings Gazette*, June 19, 1927
83 Commenting on Lindbergh's work, *Billings Gazette*, August 2, 1931
88 For years after he met Lindbergh, *Billings Gazette*, November 3, 1927

LINDBERGH IN MONTANA • 213

Chapter 12-Taking Butte by storm
90   Two Montana railroads got in the promotion act, *Helena Independent Record*, August 26, 1927
90   A few days earlier, the Great Northern Railroad, *Independent-Record*, August 24, 1927
90   The Gamer Shoe company offered, *Anaconda Standard*, September 3, 1927
91   The Home Baking Company, on Olympia Avenue, *Anaconda Standard*, September 4, 1927
91   He did not, however, grab, *Anaconda Standard*, September 4, 1927
93   "Up to the time of Lindbergh's arrival," *Anaconda Standard*, September 3, 1927
94   An estimated 40,000 people, *Idaho Statesman*, September 6, 1927
94   "Col. Charles A. Lindbergh, the thunderbird," *Anaconda Standard*, September 6, 1927
95   When Lindbergh landed in Butte, *Idaho Statesman*, September 6, 1927
95   When the *Spirit of St. Louis* touched down in Butte, *Anaconda Standard*, September 6, 1927
96   "That the throng will be representative," *Anaconda Standard*, September 5, 1927
99   That was Elmer Johnson, *Independent-Record*, September 13, 1927

Chapter 13-Great Falls gala
101 As Great Falls geared up, *Great Falls Tribune*, September 6, 1927
102 Great Falls got its moment in the Lindbergh sun, *Great Falls Tribune*, September 7, 1927

Chapter 14-Helena hubbub

105 Officials of the September 1927 event got praise, *Independent-Record*, September 4, 1927

106 The Independent Record editorialized, September 3, 1927

106 It took place during the state fair, *Wolf Point Herald*, August 26, 1927

107 After four days of "social whirl," *Great Falls Tribune*, September 9, 1927

107 She was crowned at the Lindbergh Day dinner, *Independent Record*, September 11, 1927

107 "Fair Opens With Seething Mass on Grounds," *Independent-Record*, September 6, 1927

108 When Lindbergh reached the state fairgrounds, *Independent-Record*, September 7, 1927. Continued description of the Helena event from same source.

Chapter 15-Back to Billings

115 Now, Lindbergh was a seasoned air mail pilot, *Billings Gazette*, September 8, 1927

121 Lindbergh's flight along the Yellowstone Valley, *Independent-Record*, September 17, 1927

Chapter 16-Escape into the Montana mountains

124 Lindbergh made a ground visit to Elbow Lake, *Anaconda Standard*, September 11, 1927

124 Lindbergh's whereabouts in the Swan River Valley, *Montana Standard*, September 9, 1957

126 Back in Butte, Staples reported, Charles Staples diary, Butte-Silver Bow archives

128 Seven decades after Lindbergh's visit, John Driscoll interview of Mary Katherine Staples Lynch, 1999

Chapter 17-"A thing of beauty"
131 Lindbergh took off from Butte at 11:10 a. m, *Independent-Record*, September 13, 1927
131 The mayor's question, *Missoulian*, September 11, 1927
132 Thus, Lindbergh would have time, *Missoulian*, September 12, 1927
132 Unable to honor their wish, *Missoulian*, September 13, 1927
134 One Missoula woman experienced disappointment, *Independent-Record*, September 14, 1927
134 As Lindbergh was leaving, *Anaconda Standard*, September 12, 1927
135 Lindbergh got to Spokane on time, *Anaconda Standard*, September 13, 1927
136 It sold more than 650,000 copies, Wikipedia article, viewed on June 5, 2022
136 "Slim" began his tour, *Times Union*, Brooklyn, New York, July 30, 1927
136 Lindbergh finished his trek in late October 1927, *Indianapolis Star*, October 23, 1927

Chapter 18-1928
137 A week earlier, the stage was set, *Billings Gazette*, May 20, 1928
139 The lake, about four and a half miles long, *Great Falls Tribune*, June 21, 1928
139 Ryan's son, John C. Ryan,, *Augusta*, Montana, *News*, July 12, 1928

Chapter 19-A question of loyalty

141 Lindbergh was in Missoula for about an hour, *Missoulian*, July 4, 1939

143 Their brief meeting at the Billings airport, *Laurel*, Montana, *Outlook*, July 12, 1939

144 Billings onlookers saw Lindbergh wearing, *Billings Gazette*, July 7, 1939

146 Lindbergh landed at Fargo, North Dakota, *Missoulian*, July 7, 1939

146 Thus, he was "called to the colors," *The Tennessean*, Nashville, April 19, 1939

149 It rated just Page 7 coverage, *Billings Gazette*, September 12, 1941

150 Six days after the Des Moines speech. *Billings Gazette*, September 17, 1941

152 Some years after viewing Nazi death camps, Berg

Chapter 20-War and Peace

155 Wheeler supported the declaration of war, *Billings Gazette*, December 8, 1941

155 "War, which we have tried so desperately to avoid," *Billings Gazette*, December 9, 1941

156 On one of them, a Billings man, *Billings Gazette*, December 31, 2018

Chapter 21- Casting a shadow in Montana

159 Jon and Land Lindbergh bought, *Great Falls Tribune*, April 4, 1965

139 Land Lindbergh later said, Land Lindbergh interview with author, May 22, 2022

160 He was in the company of New York Times reporter, *New York Times*, May 23, 1971

161 In 2022, Land Lindbergh, Land Lindbergh, 2022 interview

161 Lindbergh looked over the model in late 1972, *Great Falls Tribune*, December 17, 1972

163 This favorable press included an article, *Billings Gazette*, February 18, 1972

165 Billings constitutional delegate Dave Drum, *Helena Independent-Record*, February 18, 1972

145 Lindbergh's 1972 visit to Montana, *Great Falls Tribune*, February 21, 1972

166 A New York Times report published, *Great Falls Tribune*, February 4, 1972

167 Recalling the high society function, Land Lindbergh, 2022 interview

Chapter 22-Death at "my home"
172 Lindbergh had been treated for several weeks, *Billings Gazette*, August 26, 1974

Chapter 23–Still a continuing presence
176 For example, in the fall of 1987, *Missoulian*, October 18, 1988

178 In July 1988, just before the Big Sky International Air show, *Billings Gazette*, July 12, 1988

178 Residents of Billings, *Billings Gazette*, March 10, 1992

179 Great Falls residents learned in 1998, *Great Falls Tribune*, November 8, 1988

182 Further commentary on Lindbergh's flying ability, *Billings Gazette*, May 20, 2007

183 A year later, a New York City woman, *Billings Gazette*, May 9, 2008

Chapter 24-Echoes of the kidnapping in Montana
185 Montanans got another reminder of Lindbergh's life, *Montana Standard*, December 1, 2014

Conclusion
190 "A hero is someone," Joseph Campbell, *The Power of Myth*, Anchor, 1991

Index

A

Ace 17, 18, 196
Bertha Ainley 107
Canuck 71
Curtiss Jenny 71
DeHaviland 67
JN-4 56
Liberty engines 67
Lincoln Standard 7
Americus 55
Army Air Service Training Schools 67

B

E. O. Bahl 20
"Benzine Board" 72
I. O. Biffle 16
Big Horn mountains 32
Big Sky International Air show 178, 217
Billings ii, 2, 3, 6, 7, 8, 9, 10, 11, 13, 29, 30, 31, 32, 33, 35, 36, 37, 38, 41, 42, 43, 44, 45, 49, 50, 51, 52, 53, 54, 56, 58, 70, 80, 82, 83, 84, 85, 86, 87, 88, 93, 112, 114, 115, 116, 117, 118, 119, 120, 121, 124, 133, 135, 136, 137, 138, 141, 143, 144, 145, 146, 149, 150, 151, 155, 156, 164, 165, 171, 175, 177, 178, 179, 181, 182, 183, 184, 189, 190, 191, 194, 195, 203, 209, 210, 211, 212, 214, 215, 216, 217
Bird City, Kansas 27
Blackfoot River Valley 6
Bloomington, Illinois 79
Booster 6, 33, 34, 35, 39, 86, 209
Bridgeton, Missouri 75

Brooks Field 67, 71, 72
buffalo 29, 30
Butte 2, 9, 35, 36, 42, 89, 90, 91, 92, 93, 94, 95, 96, 97, 98, 99, 100, 101, 105, 106, 107, 113, 114, 116, 117, 118, 121, 123, 124, 125, 126, 127, 128, 131, 132, 133, 134, 135, 143, 165, 177, 185, 189, 190, 196, 197, 198, 204, 213, 214, 215

C

Jimmy Carter 56
Caterpillar Club 80
Central Montana Fair 9, 37
Chanute Field 17, 34, 68, 71
The Spirit of St. Louis 157
Colorado 7, 8, 25, 27, 28, 35
Contract Air Mail route 47
CAM-2 47
James Curran 23

D

Noel Davis 81
Denver 35, 36
Detroit 10, 11, 12, 55, 114, 156
Ralph Diggins 24
Dinky 53

E

Eaton ranch 30, 32
Elbow Lake 116, 123, 124, 125, 126, 127, 128, 139, 159, 198, 214

F

Fonck 81

G

Gardner 14, 16, 17
Goering 61
"goodwill tour" 135, 139, 189, 198
Great Falls 2, 9, 89, 101, 102, 103, 105, 106, 116, 124, 143, 166, 167, 177, 179, 190, 211, 213, 214, 215, 216, 217
Gurney 61, 62, 68, 69, 76

H

Harden 21, 27
Hardin 7, 30, 33, 34, 35, 89, 191, 210
Harlowton 19, 45
Helena 2, 3, 9, 35, 42, 82, 89, 90, 99, 101, 102, 103, 105, 106, 107, 108, 109, 111, 113, 114, 115, 116, 117, 118, 121, 123, 124, 128, 132, 134, 135, 143, 162, 163, 165, 167, 177, 181, 187, 189, 193, 198, 199, 200, 201, 204, 213, 214, 217
Adolf Hitler 61, 147, 150, 180, 189
H. L. Lindbourg 35
Hogan air field 8, 118
Ben Hogan 85, 119, 203
Holdredge, Nebraska 16
Homestead Business Park 37, 203

I

International Air show 68, 217

J

Louis James 22
Joyce M. Jensen 43, 211
Jovanovich 5, 6

K

Kansas 5, 7, 8, 25, 27, 37, 61
Kelly Field 17, 80, 182

Klink 71
Bill Kraske 178, 204
Kraske 50, 51, 52, 53, 54, 55, 178, 179, 195
Emil 51
Paul 36, 51

L

Lamar, Colorado 27, 28, 209
Lambert Field 68, 71, 76, 79
Lloyd Lamb 7, 37
Lewistown 2, 9, 37, 45, 46, 49, 58, 164, 211
Limon, Colorado 35, 36
Lincoln, Nebraska 5, 7, 8, 9, 13, 14, 15, 16, 17, 18, 19, 20, 21, 27, 30, 37, 41, 49, 52, 53, 55, 57, 58, 61, 62, 67, 68, 69, 70, 71, 76, 84, 86, 87, 126, 183, 194, 209
Anne Morrow 6, 25, 152, 172, 202
Lindbergh, Anne Morrow 152
Charles Lindbergh 1, 5, 10, 11, 43, 45, 46, 91, 101, 128, 138, 141, 148, 152, 159, 160, 176, 177, 178, 179, 180, 181, 183, 185, 189, 191, 193, 194, 195, 197, 198, 199, 200, 201, 203, 204
Evangeline 11
Evangeline Lindbergh 11, 55, 73, 114, 193
Jon Lindbergh 3, 6, 142, 146, 159, 160, 216
Lindbergh Lake 139, 159, 198, 202
Land Lindbergh 6, 159, 161, 165, 169, 216, 217
"dirty neck Slim" 44
Custer's Battlefield 7, 30
Little Bighorn Battlefield 7
Little Falls, Minnesota 3, 10, 11, 12, 13, 55, 64, 146, 173, 181
Love 17, 76, 115, 119, 120, 121, 132
"Cupid" 5, 8
H. J. Lynch 93
Jack Lynch 93, 191, 203
J.H. "Jack" Lynch 5

M

Maben, Mississippi 59, 60
Madison, Wisconsin 12, 13, 46, 211
Nathaniel Martin 44
Robert "Bob" Martin 44
Mathison, Mississippi 59
Meridian, Mississippi 59
Midland Empire Fair 8, 30, 32, 37, 41, 45, 210
Missoula 2, 9, 90, 91, 106, 125, 126, 127, 131, 132, 133, 134, 141, 142, 143, 145, 159, 165, 167, 177, 185, 190, 198, 202, 215, 216
Montana ii, 2, 3, 5, 6, 7, 8, 9, 10, 18, 19, 25, 27, 30, 33, 35, 37, 41, 42, 44, 45, 46, 49, 53, 55, 56, 58, 80, 87, 89, 90, 91, 93, 95, 100, 101, 105, 106, 107, 108, 109, 110, 112, 114, 115, 116, 117, 123, 124, 125, 126, 127, 128, 129, 131, 135, 137, 138, 139, 141, 143, 144, 146, 148, 150, 155, 159, 160, 161, 162, 163, 164, 165, 166, 167, 169, 171, 175, 176, 177, 178, 179, 184, 185, 189, 190, 191, 193, 194, 195, 196, 198, 199, 200, 201, 202, 209, 212, 213, 214, 215, 216, 217, 218
Monte Vista, Colorado 28
Montgomery, Alabama 59

N

Nebraska 2, 5, 7, 13, 14, 15, 16, 17, 19, 20, 25, 29, 49, 55, 62, 85, 194, 209
Nebraska Aircraft Corporation 13, 14
Thomas P. Nelson 76
Todd Nelson 30
Charles Nungesser 82

O

Orteig Prize 81
Raymond Orteig 81

Ottawa, Illinois 78

P

Page 15, 17, 18
Ray Page 15, 20
Pallas 52
Peoria, Illinois 76, 77
pickling plant 44

R

Red Lodge 37, 83, 84, 164
O.L. "Shorty" Reese 37
Reese 56
Carl Riddick 46
Merrill Riddick 46
Riddick 46, 47
Rinehart 30, 31, 32
Robertson Aircraft Corporation 47, 75
Robertson 77
William Robertson 76
Rogers 5, 27
Rowand 31, 32

S

San Antonio 67, 72
Savage, Minnesota 63, 64
Scala 43, 210
Shakopee, Minnesota 63
Shea 84, 85
Shoemaker 31, 32, 120
Sidney 19
Spencer, Frank 44
Spirit 91, 94, 101, 102
Spirit of St. Louis 1, 5, 9, 81, 84, 90, 91, 95, 98, 102, 106, 107,

111, 117, 118, 119, 121, 123, 157, 161, 162, 165, 171, 181, 182, 190, 197, 198, 199, 213
Springfield, Illinois 76, 77
St. Louis 77, 78, 79, 80

T

Roy Thompson 23
Thompson's 23
Timm 19, 61
Treasure State i, ii, 2, 6, 33, 89, 105, 106, 107, 108, 117, 123, 125, 160, 161, 167, 185, 189, 191, 210

U

University of Wisconsin 5, 12
UW 12, 13

W

C. A. Warner 43
Wedron, Illinois 78
Bob Westover 3, 30, 37, 42, 82, 115, 117, 119, 143, 183, 184, 203, 210
Ed Westover 30, 87, 195
Wooster 81
Wyoming 7, 8, 25, 29, 30, 31, 37, 184

www.ingramcontent.com/pod-product-compliance
Lightning Source LLC
Chambersburg PA
CBHW071236070526
44583CB00017B/2204